'A terrific account of dinghy sailing and seafaring adventure, spanning almost 50 years from exuberant youth to seasoned yachtsman. Peter tells and beautifully illustrates his story. He has demonstrated in photos and images the versatility and suitability of the Wayfarer dinghy for fun, family, and fantastic adventure.'

RICHARD AND MARK HARTLEY
t builders

'In conveying the very real dangers of offshore sailing in a small open boat, and the level of planning, preparation, determination and seamanship, not to say sheer luck, required to succeed, the book could hardly be bettered.'

RICHARD WYNNE
Nautical editor, UK

'An object lesson in how to turn dreams into reality, of how to complete extremely risky challenges through careful preparation, constant vigilance and willingness to adapt a plan once under way.'

BRIAN THOMPSON
Professional ocean racing Grand Prix sailor

'The stories in this book capture the essence of everything that is small open boat sailing. This book is an enjoyable read which can spur on the adventurous and entertain the rest.'

JOHN MELLOR
Chairman, UK Wayfarer Class Association

'The events described, and the hardships not described, are so extreme as to seem suicidal.'

JOHN MARDALL
Maritime editor, Florida

THE SEA TAKES NO PRISONERS

THE SEA TAKES NO PRISONERS

Offshore Voyages in an Open Dinghy

PETER CLUTTERBUCK

RD COLES NAUTICAL

OMSBURY

ORD · NEW YORK · NEW DELHI · SYDNEY

Adlard Coles Nautical
An imprint of Bloomsbury Publishing Plc

50 Bedford Square
London
WC1B 3DP
UK

1385 Broadway
New York
NY 10018
USA

www.bloomsbury.com
www.adlardcoles.com

ADLARD COLES, ADLARD COLES NAUTICAL and the Buoy logo
are trademarks of Bloomsbury Publishing Plc

First Bloomsbury edition 2018

First published 2015

British Library Cataloguing-in-Publication Data
A catalogue record for this book is available from the British Library.

Library of Congress Cataloguing-in-Publication data has been applied for.

ISBN: PB: 978-1-4729-4571-6
ePDF: 978-1-4729-4570-9
ePub: 978-1-4729-4569-3

2 4 6 8 10 9 7 5 3 1

Original text edited by Hugh Brazier
Maps by Louis Mackay / www.louismackaydesign.com

Typeset in Fournier by Deanta Global Publishing Services, Chennai, India
Printed and bound in Great Britain by Bell & Bain Ltd, Glasgow

To find out more about our authors and books visit www.bloomsbury.com.
Here you will find extracts, author interviews, details of forthcoming events
and the option to sign up for our newsletters.

AUTHOR'S NOTE: The information in this book may supplement but not replace
proper sailing training. Offshore sailing poses inherent risk, and can be especially
hazardous in open dinghies. Be sure that your boat and equipment are well maintained
and do not take risks beyond your level of experience, aptitude, training and comfort level.

Contents

Maps

This book is dedicated to those who shared *Calypso*'s greatest adventures:

George Greenwood, Barry Hunt-Taylor, Peter Jesson and Tom Moore;

and to my father, who introduced me to sailing

Voyages of the Wayfarer *Calypso*, 1964–2005.

Foreword

BY BRIAN THOMPSON

Back in the 1960s and 1970s, voyaging was far more perilous than now – there was no GPS navigation, no AIS collision avoidance system. Weather forecasts were far less precise and reliable than now. And of course communication devices were almost non-existent, with no VHF handhelds and no mobile phones – a call box in a foreign port was about the most high tech system available to a voyager in a Wayfarer dinghy.

It was a different time, and maybe because of the freedom from technology, it brought a freedom from oversight and a huge measure of unpredictability. It would be hard to imagine a pair of teenagers being allowed to undertake such open boat voyages now!

Peter, in his very immediate narration, brings those youthful adventures back to life, and makes them read like they happened just last summer.

These voyages are an object lesson in how to turn dreams into reality: of how to complete extremely risky challenges through careful preparation, constant vigilance, and willingness to adapt a plan once underway.

Few people would have been driven, organised and skilled enough to be able to act on this dream, and fewer still could overcome all the obstacles to make each trip successful.

Having sailed with Peter in the 1990s on racing trimarans around Britain and to the Azores, it's been a revelation to me that he had done these amazing adventures so long before, and had kept these stories locked away. I am very glad that they are in book form now, to inspire new generations of adventurers to go exploring in small boats.

Brian Thompson

Brian became the first Briton to break the round the world sailing record twice, and the first to sail non-stop around the world four times. He has broken 27 sailing world records. He has sailed in major solo ocean races, including the OSTAR race, the Route du Rhum and the Vendée Globe non-stop Round the World Race.

Preface

I have always been inspired by tales of adventure, and that is part of the reason for this book: to share some exciting voyages that I've had the good fortune to make. As a boy, I read incessantly of voyages to far-off places – the travels of Magellan, Drake and Cook – and I was forever intrigued by the thrill of finding a port after a tough sea crossing. Storms at sea, huge breaking waves, black starless nights and the beauty of rugged coastlines beckoned me to live the experience. My dream job would have been skipper of a clipper ship, a century earlier. Some of my ancestors were Vikings, and they had settled in the Outer Hebrides. Maybe there was salt in the family's blood.

This book is mostly about some long voyages I made in the late 1960s in my Wayfarer dinghy *Calypso*. I was asked to write these up at the time for *Yachting World* magazine, which published a series of articles. These voyages were believed to be the longest recorded in a class dinghy – some 1,200 miles in two cases. A lot of dangerous incidents took place, partly because I ventured into conditions my boat was not designed for, but mainly because I was an inexperienced teenage sailor, learning from my mistakes. Recently, many people have said that I should write a book about these voyages, and the question that always comes up is 'why did you do it?' The simple answer is that it was a thirst for adventure combined with insatiable curiosity. It was also the cheapest means of travel for me as a student, because my free hotel room came with me to each anchorage or port. I could live for three months on £50.

What has changed in the 45 years since then? The sea has not. It is still a dangerous place which does not forgive errors. I have changed, in that I would not now take the risks that I looked forward to when I was full of the buoyancy of youth. Another change is that technology has made offshore sailing much safer. In the 1960s we had no GPS, no EPIRBs, no mobile phones, no way of calling for help. We navigated mainly by sextant and compass. Boats and fittings were not as strong as they are today. *Calypso* was made of plywood, which sometimes split in two when we hit a big wave. Fittings were mostly bronze. Things broke often. Plenty went wrong: a dismasting, two capsizes, nine rudder breakages, getting lost and arriving at islands we mistook for others.

Dinghies are still not a safe means of transport on the open sea: no keel, so easily capsized; no cabin, so no shelter from foul weather; no motor, so no means of propulsion other than oars when unable to sail; no electricity for navigation or lights. When I started dinghy cruising, there were no marinas, and usually we had to anchor overnight. There were also very few yachts, as yachting was mainly for the rich elite.

The world has become more sanitised and risk-averse. I now need a licence to charter a yacht in the Croatian islands. I also need a VHF licence. I am often obliged to wear a lifejacket in a flat calm. I have to sign lots of agreements and disclaimers when I go sailing. If I repeated the trips now, they would be safer, with more experience behind me, better equipment, and information gained in advance from the internet. But some of the raw adventure, the magic of surprise, the venturing into the unknown, would be lost.

An open boat gives you an intimacy with the sea that sailors in seagoing sailing vessels are insulated from. You cannot escape from its power. Asleep on the floorboards, the spray would still be flying, and the worry of a capsize still there. Trust was essential, or sleep would never come. We did many overnight passages, up to three days non-stop in the Atlantic, and fatigue was a huge risk. Dropping off to sleep whilst helming, and the crew asleep, could lead to a gybe or a capsize.

And the positives? The thrill of picking up a big wave and surfing it. Phosphorescence breaking over the decks into the boat and swilling around inside. Shooting stars. Dolphins leaping a few feet from us, and way above our heads. Cliffs by the light of the moon. The first light of dawn after a long, cold night. Safe landfall after a crisis at sea. I also did these trips to try to become a better person: to appreciate the beauty of the planet, to be able to suffer hardship, to solve difficult problems, to build courage, to learn the moods of the sea, to stretch myself beyond my limits. I thought that this would help me deal with the challenges that would come my way in my sailing, career, and personal life.

After the cruises of the 1960s, I went on to a sailing career full of variety: as a professional yachtsman, a US Coast Guard licensed captain, and a sailing instructor in the USA, later crossing the Atlantic and Pacific Oceans, including taking part in the Singlehanded Transpacific Race. Brian Thompson joined me to campaign my 43-foot offshore Grand Prix racing trimaran *Spirit of England* to fifteen wins and four international race records, mostly in Atlantic waters. I produced *The Sixty Minute Sailor*, a learn-to-sail video, filmed in California on board the same Wayfarer that is the subject of this book. For a few years I worked offshore on the North Sea oil rigs, and once experienced a hurricane force 12 storm in midwinter at 62 degrees north. The waves, some 60 feet high, would have crushed most large yachts. A dinghy at sea is in the lap of the gods above force 6.

In a dinghy, the risks were greater, the sea was closer, the weather had more impact, and the need to focus on every minute detail was ever-present. At every stage, the situation controlled our responses, reminding us that the sea was always the master, and that it took no prisoners.

I still sail *Calypso*, but now I sail her with my family, 50 years after my first voyage in her. Recent trips have taken me around the Fastnet Rock and to the Scilly Isles. I've owned many boats – dinghies, yachts and multihulls – but the only one that I still have is the Wayfarer. The Wayfarer taught me how to sail, and the boat is timeless. It was, and still is, a brilliant design by Ian Proctor.

Over the years I've had so much fun, adventure and enjoyment aboard *Calypso* that it gives me great pleasure to know that the Wayfarer is enjoying a resurgence in popularity under the steward-ship of the new builders: Hartley Boats, in Derbyshire. The Hartley team have taken a very personal interest in the boat, in the Wayfarer Class Association, and in the way in which ordinary people want to sail this extraordinary boat. Together with the renowned yacht designer Phil Morrison, they have redesigned the hull and layout to make it a safer, stronger, more attractive and far more comfort-able boat in which to sail and adventure. I wish them every success in building and supplying Wayfarers for years to come. In doing so they will help others like me to experience and enjoy wonderful adventure.

Part 1

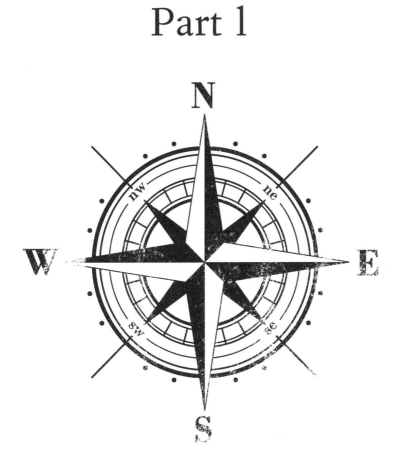

Prologue

Peter Jesson and I were sailing a 16-foot plywood dinghy across the Bay of Biscay, out of sight of land. We were about 20 miles off the French coast, preparing to sail on through the night. But something was not right. Peter was normally unflappable, but he looked worried. I was very worried indeed, but hoped Peter would not notice my fears.

He asked loudly, above the moaning roar of the rising wind, 'What's going to happen? The weather's going to get really bad soon. We need to decide what to do.'

'Trying to assess our options. This swell is telling us that bad weather is coming.'

The sky was black to the west, and it looked like a huge, menacing squall. This had every aspect of the Atlantic in an ugly mood. The shipping forecast was imminent, so we hove to. I unstowed our waterproof radio direction finder and tuned in. But all I could hear was crackling noises. When sea area Biscay came up, I heard only one word: 'seven'. Our little boat would not survive a force seven.

I gave the radio to Peter to re-stow, and set the boat back to sailing on a beam reach. The black sky was upon us. White foam was being blown off the waves as the wind picked up to our weather side. Suddenly, it hit us. We were knocked down, and I let the sheets fly on both sails. The sails were flogging uncontrollably now, and shaking the boat violently. I could not luff up, as the wind was too strong. I dared not bear away, as we would take off like a rocket out of control. We could not stay as we were – we would be blown over, and we could never right the boat in such conditions. Night was coming. If we capsized, we would either be wrecked or die of hypothermia.

The seas were getting rapidly bigger, and the wind was blowing the tops off the waves in sheets of white spume. The noise went to a high-pitched shriek. What choices did we have?

The western horizon was still darkening and the rest of the sky was becoming uglier every minute. We had to get out of this.

At 1850 we bore away and *Calypso* began surfing down the steepening waves in the fading light towards Île de Pilier, which guarded the north end of Noirmoutier. Soon we were surfing up waves as well. *Calypso* was in danger of driving her bows under, or being pooped by the large seas. The wind was rising inexorably. I was expecting the jib to be split in two any moment. The sky was black to windward, above us were red streaks of cirrus, and to the south it was a sickly green and yellow. Soon, some ragged brown clouds scudded low overhead and the rain began as the light faded. It was a frightening sky.

Calypso was planing continuously up and down waves like a speed-boat under only 46 square feet of canvas, and the safety line on the rudder blade was screaming. We could not risk going any closer to the rocks. We had to try to beat off them now. Everything depended on being able to sail to windward into the lee of the island. It was dark now. The sea was breaking around us on rocks and shallows. Ahead were more breakers. We had to turn and try to beat. Would the trysail adaptor work? Could we escape the rocks downwind of us? Could we control the boat on this stormy night? Would we be able to see the lighthouse and its white sector light? Could we point high enough to get to the beach? Would we capsize? Or hit a rock? We were driving through sheets of spray in the howling wind, and the self-bailer was working overtime. The rain was by now heavy and pelting horizontally. What chance did we have?

Learning the Ropes

Broads and rivers

In 1964, my father decided to buy a second-hand Wayfarer dinghy for the family, at a cost of £250. The boat had been owned by Crab Searle, who ran the Emsworth Sailing School on Chichester Harbour. Searle was a retired Royal Air Force group captain, who got his nickname in World War II from flying biplanes and skidding sideways to land, or to avoid enemy fire. My father and I drove to Emsworth, and there she was – blue hull, white painted decks, just under 16 feet long. She was a big dinghy, built of plywood over a wooden frame.

The Wayfarer had a number of features that distinguished it from other sailing dinghies. It was larger and heavier than most. It had buoyancy compartments in the bows and stern, within which gear could be stowed dry. It was big enough for you to sling a canvas across the boom and camp underneath it. It had a mast that pivoted at deck level, so that it could be lowered whilst at sea, or for going under bridges.

Frank Dye had sailed a Wayfarer called *Wanderer* from the north of Scotland to Iceland in the summer of 1963. This was an amazing feat in a boat designed for sheltered waters. He then sailed from Scotland across the northern North Sea to Norway in 1964. This time, he was caught in a force 8–9 gale, and had to lower the mast and lie to a drogue made of the mainsail and boom, as the storm built. However, the seas were too big, and the boat was rolled and driven

Learning on the Broads.

under four times, smashing the mast into small pieces. When they were rolled, they were driven deep underwater as 30-foot waves crashed over them. They were pulling in 45 feet of warp with each wave every fifteen seconds to try to keep head to sea. Much gear was lost overboard, and the rest was saturated with sea water. These voyages made Frank a legend as people read about them in the media. However, they also convinced my father that the design was sturdy, and would be a good boat for me to develop sailing skills, which he saw as the ability to plan expeditions, survive the elements, and lead men out of hazards. I got foul weather gear, a knife with a marlin spike, and sea boots. I was ready for adventure!

Our first sail was during the end of a snowy English winter. It was pure magic – beating along chilly estuaries in blustery winds, running under a red spinnaker across the wide open waters at Chichester Harbour, initially with my father, then with boys and girls at the sailing school.

I rigged up the tent to try out the camping setup, and dressed up for a cold night out in the garden at our house in Berkhamsted with

Sailing with my father, Richard, who got me started.

four heavy jersey sweaters over my normal winter clothes. There was ice in the boat overnight, but I survived, sleeping on an air mattress on the boat's floorboards.

At the end of the winter we then towed the boat to Oulton Broad on the Norfolk Broads, where my father had sailed in his youth. The Broads are a collection of rivers and lakes, all tidal. Strong currents and narrow rivers demanded a set of skills that had framed the early development of legendary sailors such as Lord Nelson. We had a small cooker, 30 garbage bags for keeping things dry, and some dark green army kitbags. We sailed a few days along the rivers, and I learned my father's wartime camping techniques, which he had perfected over four years in tents across Africa, Italy and Germany. Aluminium mess tins were used for storing food, then for washing and shaving, then as cooking pots, then to eat out of, then as washing-up bowls, using copious quantities of newspaper to scrub down the burned-on cooking remnants. My father left, so that I then became 'captain', and I was joined by a friend from school, Patrick McCartney.

We were both fourteen and we learned fast. Often we could not sail against the forces of wind and current as we strived to reach

Getting under way.

a mooring by nightfall. We tried to paddle, but the boat was too big to paddle at any speed, and we ended up being pushed back by the tidal currents. We tried towing the boat, with one of us on the bank pulling a long rope and the other steering to keep off the mud banks along the river edge, but often the rope would get caught in the reeds, or the boat would run into the mud because the rope was never quite long enough, or whoever was on the bank would be obstructed by tidal creeks, and end up covered in mud. A couple of times we just moored up in the dark wherever we got to, and spent miserable nights in the mud along the edge of the water.

Road traffic crossed these rivers by chain ferry, and we had to be careful to avoid the submerged chains. Railways crossed on swing bridges, which opened as you sailed up to them, unless a train was coming. Once we saw a yacht out of control in strong winds hit one of these bridges when it stayed closed, shearing the mast right off ten feet above the deck amidst much panic and shouting from the crew.

8

On Oulton Broad.

In the summer, I went out for another expedition cruise on the Broads, this time with Dana Prescott, the eldest son of an American military family that we had known in Fort Leavenworth, Kansas. We had strong winds, and gale forecasts many days. One day, the mast broke and crashed over the side.

What to do now? We had to get to a place where we could haul the boat out. We would have to sail downwind, and to do that we needed another mast. Our mast was useless, lashed along the decks. Dana was a strong American teenager. He became a human mast, holding a spinnaker pole up with the jib as our sole sail. We sailed back as far as we could, downwind only, and eventually reached a ramp where we could haul the boat out.

Dana Prescott.

Hard preparations

Later in the year my father towed the boat to the west coast of Scotland, where my brother Robin and I sailed with him on the open sea for the first time. We were camped at a village called Plockton, near the Isle of Skye, where half the inhabitants were called Mackenzie. We raced against the local dinghies and fishing boats in crystal-clear water, through which we could see granite rocks slipping by underneath us. Grey mountains and grey seas surrounded us on the bad-weather days. On the drive back south, a big storm came down and the boat filled with rainwater, which caused the trailer to break in two from the extra weight. My father was very resourceful from his wartime days, and able to fix most things by lashing up repairs with ropes. This he did, and the trailer was on the move again. We bucketed out the water periodically to keep the boat as light as possible.

When winter came, I decided to repaint the boat and change a few fittings. First I had to break up the ice that had set in the bilges. We moved the boat to a remote farm barn and turned her over. I spent days stripping the paint off, in freezing conditions down to −5 °C. The paint was so thick at these temperatures that I had to stand the paint cans in a cook pot of warm water. It was hard work, but I was passionate about the boat, which I was beginning to manage as if she were my own. Other than my father, none of the others in my family showed much interest in her.

I could see bigger and bigger adventures coming along. I spent days in sub-zero temperatures, gloves and hats on, working on what I saw as my chariot to freedom. This was my escape from the drudgery and discipline of a British boarding school. It was my passport to far-off places. It used no fuel, did not need a ticket, and provided a home under a tent over the boom, free of charge. There was no cheaper way of travelling. And although I didn't appreciate this aspect until years later, a sailing boat leaves no carbon footprint on its voyages. It was a green machine.

The following April I went sailing again on the Broads with George Greenwood. George was a friend from school who lived a

At Plockton, on the west coast of Scotland.

half-hour's bike ride from our Berkhamsted house. He was legendary at school for his fearless goalkeeping, usually returning from a match completely encased in mud and looking more like a First World War soldier after a day's combat in the trenches. He was a passionate sailor and already had some experience of crewing ocean racers. He also had a tough and resilient personality. On our first night, a strong wind blew up and the boat broke loose, drifting across and down the river, with the tent still up. We were washed up in a pile of reeds on the mud bank in a dark night. At daybreak, we stowed the tent and paddled back. The wind gusted to a strong force 6 during the day, and we almost capsized, taking on board some 300 gallons of water. George was a very experienced and capable sailor, and I could trust him in difficult conditions. In strong winds we kept full sail up so that we could lift up and plane like a speedboat.

We were two fifteen-year-olds having the time of our lives. Curiosity, and testing our limits, overruled any sense of fear. Nights were still cold at this time of year, and I slept inside my sleeping bag wearing all my day clothes, plus three heavy sweaters.

When the wind and tide were against us, it was often impossible to make headway by sailing, or paddling, as we did not have oars. We still had to man-haul the boat by towing it from the river bank. We did the same when there was no wind, or if we had the sails and mast down for the bridges. Often we got under the bridges by standing on the deck and pulling ourselves along by grabbing the girders underneath.

In August, my father rented a tiny attic room for me to stay in at a yacht club on the Solent, and I kept the boat there. This was an amazing experience, living for four weeks as a cadet amongst the wealthy upper classes. One day a launch arrived with the Duke of Edinburgh and Princess Anne aboard, and I was ordered to carry their suitcases from the dock. The sailing was fantastic, and I often made the trip with friends over to the Isle of Wight and back, planing fast in the strong winds. I got some really adventurous sailing, with waves up to eight feet high. We would slam into these, barely able to make any headway, with the mainsail reefed down to a 'pocket handkerchief'. Sailing with the waves was electric, surfing at break-neck speed. On one of these days, the tiller broke and I lost my crew overboard. I managed to get him back, as fortunately we were in sheltered waters.

In September George joined me again and we sailed east along the coast to Chichester Harbour. On the way back, a gale came down, and we ran back to Hamble with just the tiny jib up in howling winds and heavy rain from the south-east. In the Hamble River, the moored yachts were being pounded by big waves, and the wind was shrieking in the rigging. On the radio, we heard that the wind had built to force 10, and there were 30-foot waves off Chichester. We'd got back just in time.

That winter, I was doing labouring jobs building farm sheds with George. It was back-breaking working, hauling heavy sacks of cement, but it built up muscle as well as cash for the boat. We yearned for more adventurous sailing in the open sea. I bought a compass and a pump. I got a small parachute sea anchor made, which we could set in the open sea off a long warp, and thereby lie head to wind in gales, or make repairs if something broke. I was desperately short of money, and had to juggle between boat costs and the rest of my expenses. I hitchhiked as much as possible to avoid the cost of trains. To save money, we planned to sleep ashore in bus shelters during our cruise. I was not able to earn enough from my labour-ing jobs, and had to watch every penny. I wrote dozens of letters to equipment suppliers pleading for discounts.

I had never been in truly open sea in anything smaller than a channel ferry, so I thought it wise to arrange a cruise in company with another dinghy, but could not find anyone willing to take their boat out into the exposed waters off the south coast of England. My father had seen sailing as a means to develop organisational and leadership skills. My shortcomings in these areas were imme-diately apparent.

To get the boat ready for the open sea, there was a tremendous amount of correspondence and fitting out to do, further complicated by the fact that my parents were by now abroad, living in a Singapore Army Compound. I had no access to a vehicle for moving the boat except from my uncle, John Clutterbuck, a schoolmaster with a naval career which had included an active role in the sinking of the *Bismarck*. He helped us no end.

I visited the legendary Frank Dye in 1966. I had written to him asking if he could give me any advice by post on a few problems I had had in fitting out the boat, which I had now named *Calypso*, for sea passages. He invited me to stay overnight, which was very kind and hospitable of him and very valuable for me. I hitchhiked to his home in Norfolk, where I also met his wife Margaret. Margaret later pursued a dinghy cruising career of her own. I was very touched that such a famous man would be so hospitable. He was quiet, with a steely calmness about him. He explained how to heave to, setting the jib to windward, with the main flapping loose, and the tiller lashed to leeward, so that the boat would be self-tending. The helmsman could then leave the tiller and do such things as reefing or navigation, even while the crew was asleep on the windward-side floorboards. Frank and Margaret wrote books on these voyages ten years later, and they still make gripping reading.

Packing everything in

I was planning to go to sea, but *Calypso* was not capable of what I wanted her to do without some modifications. I decided to build a new stowage layout. Previously we had stowed nearly all the gear in the bow and stern buoyancy compartments. This was unsatisfactory, as it was rather inaccessible, and a lot of structural strain was put on the boat because of the weight concentrated at each end. This would not be good if we were caught out in big seas. So the layout was altered so that all gear likely to be needed when under way (such as a radio for weather forecasts, first aid kit, food, charts, sea anchor,

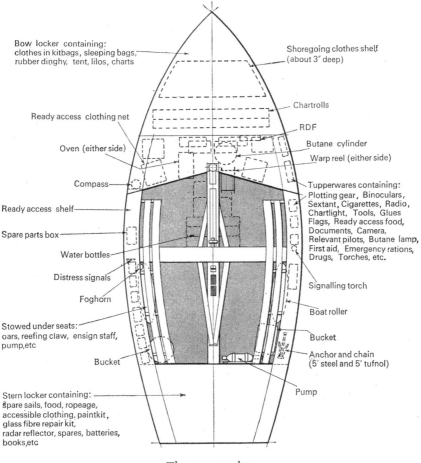

Bow locker containing:
clothes in kitbags, sleeping bags,
rubber dinghy, tent, lilos, charts

Shoregoing clothes shelf
(about 3″ deep)

Chartrolls

Ready access clothing net

RDF

Oven (either side)

Butane cylinder

Warp reel (either side)

Compass

Tupperwares containing:
Plotting gear, Binoculars,
Sextant, Cigarettes, Radio,
Chartlight, Tools, Glues
Flags, Ready access food,
Documents, Camera,
Relevant pilots, Butane lamp,
First aid, Emergency rations,
Drugs, Torches, etc.

Ready access shelf

Spare parts box

Water bottles

Distress signals

Signalling torch

Foghorn

Boat roller

Stowed under seats:
oars, reefing claw, ensign staff,
pump, etc

Bucket

Bucket

Anchor and chain
(5′ steel and 5′ tufnol)

Stern locker containing:
spare sails, food, ropeage,
accessible clothing, paintkit,
glass fibre repair kit,
radar reflector, spares, batteries,
books, etc

Pump

The stowage plan.

paddles, pliers) was stowed in the cockpit in clips or stowage nets or lashed down in one of eight watertight containers. In practice, we very rarely had to open a hatch to gain access to the watertight compartments at sea. It was not a good idea to open these at sea, as if a wave filled them up we would lose the essential buoyancy to keep the boat stable and upright if swamped.

Also, if we did capsize, I wanted to make sure that most things were still attached to the boat, rather than floating away. I loaded *Calypso* stern-heavy so as to reduce the risk of a dangerous broach, and to help the bows rise to big seas. We had over 150 items of gear, about ten times the number of items needed for the day sailing that the Wayfarer was intended for. This list was to expand to over 500 items within three years when we took on open-ocean sailing.

I planned for many emergencies: dismasting, being holed, smashed on a lee shore, and so on. We carried copper sheets for repairing holes, and loads of tools and fittings for repairs at sea. I was confident enough of our sailing skills not to expect a capsize, but this could easily occur if a big sea flipped us, or a rope jammed, or we got too fatigued. Righting the boat in big waves would be impossible. In the worst case, we hoped to be able to abandon ship and swim for shore. Capsize was a serious risk, and my biggest fear was the mainsheet being tangled around gear on the floorboards. We had to keep everything tidy, so that ropes would not tangle and everything could be found in the dark. The mainsheet had to be able to be released at all times in a fraction of a second, day or night. Luffing up was another option, but not much good in big seas or strong winds – we would still be blown over.

We would have to be like tightrope walkers, concentrating on balance day and night, fully aware of the consequence of relaxing our vigilance. There was no heavy keel below our dinghy to keep us from flipping over. Another risk was an accidental gybe while the crew was off-watch asleep on the weather-side floorboards. The crew would then be on the lee side, with his weight encouraging a capsize. If we went over, he would probably be drowned, trapped under the thwart. At night this was a real risk, especially when we were exhausted. The chance of a capsize at night was also much greater, owing to fatigue, loss of sense of direction, undetected rope jams, and inability to see windshifts or waves. A fraction of a second dozing off could lead to a disaster: a gybe, a tack, and a subsequent capsize.

With everything made ready, we decided to head west to Weymouth. I longed for the adventure of the high seas. The chief danger on this coastline is the area of overfalls near St Alban's

Ledge. There are various tidal races, notably the Peverell Ledge/ Anvil Point Race which was later to overwhelm us, and other potentially dangerous areas such as the Needles Channel and Chichester Bar. I was very apprehensive about each of these so spent some time working out the most favourable conditions for each obstacle. My father wrote to me from Singapore advising me not to attempt some of these areas, as he had been nearly overwhelmed in a seagoing yacht at St Alban's in the tide rip there, with boiling seas breaking over all the decks.

Being a teenager and thousands of miles from him, I only took what advice I chose to. It was Mark Twain who said, 'When I was a boy of fourteen, my father was so ignorant I could hardly stand to have the old man around. But when I got to be twenty-one, I was astonished at how much the old man had learned in seven years.' Teenage boys don't change much over the generations. In retrospect, my father's advice was always good. He regarded the sea as a fearsome place, where breakages and storms were always threatening. He had been wrecked himself in a gale, when anchors gave way and he was badly injured as chains ripped out. We were to have loads of breakages and crises over the next three years. We were lucky to get away with it.

I was pumped up with curiosity. How would our little dinghy fare in the big waves and open sea that I craved?

2

Venturing to the Open Sea

Out to sea

On Wednesday 27 July 1966, George and I launched *Calypso* and sailed 15 miles west down the Solent against the flooding tide, from Hamble to Keyhaven. There, in an isolated area of mudflats and marshes, a local barman offered to keep an eye on the boat in case it drifted away in the night. He was an extraordinary red-bearded seaman, known locally as Sinbad. He travelled on a tricycle and preferred to sleep outside with his two dogs – as 'there's lots of funny things going on around here at night.' I tried out our tiny rubber dinghy, but it refused to go in any direction except round in circles, being driven by one paddle only. I took a short walk westwards to the beach, where breakers were announcing our planned journey into the open sea. I eagerly awaited the next day's adventures.

Next morning we left at 0825 and headed west through the Needles Channel, on a strong turbulent tide rip into open waters. This was a dream come true. The horizon changed to a flat open grey line where the sea met the sky. Outside, we put on oilskins, life-jackets and safety harnesses. We prepared for our first taste of sea.

The wind was rising, so I clambered onto the foredeck to change the foresail. George came off watch after four hours at 1220 and soon we had crossed the wide bay to Poole Harbour. Being short of cash, we looked for the cheapest overnight accommodation. We asked at the police station to see if they could lend us a couple of cells, but they

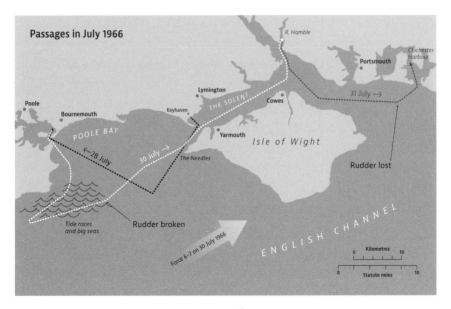

Passages in July 1966.

declined. In the end, I slept in *Calypso*, which necessitated patching a large tear in the tent, and George slept in an outboard motor shed.

The 0640 shipping forecast on 29 July was wind up to force 6. We planned to take St Alban's Head at slack water at 1545, when the dangerous tide rips and overfalls would be at rest. This meant going outside the Handfast Point and Anvil Point tide races, which would be creating violent waves and swirling waters on a spring ebb stream. The wind was SW force 5, so we put seven rolls into the mainsail to reduce its size by half and hoisted the small jib. When we were out of the lee of Handfast Point, the wind was WSW and force 6, so we dropped the jib. The seas were gradually getting larger as we sailed south, and by 1330 we were out of the lee of Durlston Head with America the nearest land to windward of us.

The seas grew as we went further out into the open sea until they were truly huge. George was sitting out at the front of the cockpit, trying to keep the boat upright with his body weight, hanging onto the shroud so as not to be swept off.

'Watch out, Peter, some really big ones ahead.'

Calypso's bows lifted as we were drawn up a steep wall of water. A crest was curling over to land on us. It hit *Calypso* and George like a rugby scrum, knocking us back and breaking over the boat, then into the cockpit, half filling it.

'We've got to pump it out fast!' I yelled. George was pumping as hard as he could, but the pump was not able to keep up with the amount of water coming in. I grabbed the bucket.

'Hang on, another big one,' I warned George. It broke in, and then we were on top of the wave as it roared underneath us. We crashed into the bottom and stopped dead. There was no wind down here, but I could hear it roaring overhead.

'Another big one, must be as high as the mast,' shouted George. He looked worried, much as I remembered him as a goalkeeper: ready for an onslaught, alert, adrenaline rushing, putting fear behind him. We were slammed again, and while on top I could see the cliffs to our right.

'White breakers ahead.' George was pointing. 'Worse than here.'

'Can't be worse – these are very dangerous right here!' I shouted back.

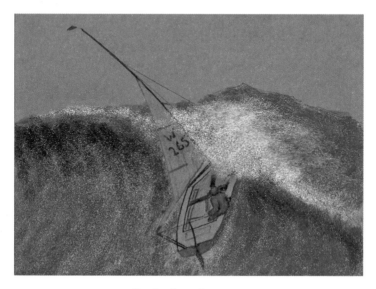

Beating into giant seas.

Then I saw what he had seen. There was a line of white water extending from the cliffs out to where we were going, and with every wave it grew closer. I remembered that the tide would be pulling us into this.

'Is this a tide race?' George was questioning. He looked very worried now.

'The boat can't handle any more than this,' I said. The mast was 22 feet high. The waves were about that big, but it wasn't the height that worried me, it was their steepness. They were black on their steep faces, white on top, and white where breakers had left a trail of spray.

'We should go back,' George demanded.

But could we? *Calypso* would be running with the waves and surfing them. They were moving so fast, we'd be out of control.

'I can't turn back here,' I said. 'It's too dangerous.'

'And it's too dangerous to carry on,' he replied.

I was fighting to overcome increasing fear. The sea was roaring. The air was shrieking. We had no place being here. There were no other boats out here. No one could rescue us. We had to be very careful. The waves were tipping *Calypso* over as they hit us.

'I'm going to raise the centreboard,' George volunteered. 'Maybe we'll be tipped less when we're broadsided.'

He raised it up halfway. Another breaker hit us near the top of the next wave. We slipped sideways instead of being rolled. But there was another problem: to take on the biggest breakers, we needed to luff into them and split them apart with our bows, reducing the amount of water coming in. With the board up, we could not do this, and we were exposed to them breaking over the side decks.

'We're never going to be able to beat to weather,' I warned.

'If we go much further, we'll get close to the race off St Alban's Head,' George yelled back. 'The seas could be monumental there.' He was pumping flat out.

The problem was removing the water faster than it came in. We were being tossed about like a toy in a washing machine. The power and the roar of the sea was terrifying. This was beyond an adventure – it was turning into a nightmare, potentially a disaster. I was mesmerised by the phenomenal roar of the breaking seas.

There was another factor which scared me. I had seen some huge breakers curling over and crashing like big waves on a beach, but they had miraculously landed either side of us. What would happen if one landed on top of us? *Calypso* could be crushed. Or we could be carried over with the lip of the breaker and smashed as we dropped with it to the trough.

Mighty waves

The sea was a mass of huge white breakers. And with each passing minute the waves grew ever bigger and steeper as the tide ripped into the dark Atlantic rollers. *Calypso* could be flipped over at any moment, and we would never be able to right her in these giant waves. The tide would then sweep us further out into the grey, open, boiling sea.

'We've got to go back,' I yelled at George. We had to turn back before we had a fatal accident. George dropped the main and raised the jib, which was now all we had up. I hoped we would not surf out of control on the faces of these big, near-vertical seas. It was now force 7, gale strength. We had to get back to land, fast, before it got any worse, and before we were rolled. We could never right the boat in such big waves. No one knew where we were, and no one would know we were in trouble.

I pulled the tiller in between waves and bore her around until the wind was behind us. *Calypso* rode before the wind under jib alone. I looked astern. A huge wave was towering behind us. I had to take it square on, or we'd be rolled over. We sometimes shipped water over the side decks, and I feared being pooped by a wave breaking over the stern. The steepest waves would pick *Calypso* up and throw her forward with bows down and out of the water as far as the after end of the centreboard case, at breakneck speed.

This exhilarating surf ride would last maybe ten seconds, then *Calypso*'s bows would point up as the crest frothed underneath and we would glide down the back of the wave. Sometimes, a wave would tower behind us with a curler that looked as if it was going to land right on top of us, but the boat would start surfing down the wave front, and then the wave would break and we'd be sailing on air in the froth of the breaker.

Once round Handfast Point, the cliffs protected us from the seas. We hardened up but could not make any progress into the wind, so reefed the mainsail until only the top batten was in, and hoisted it, about a quarter of its full size. Even then *Calypso* was frequently overpowered. We arrived back at Poole Harbour, shaken and relieved. The gale was screaming through the rigging of the boats in the harbour. Trees were being whipped back and forth in the gusts.

'Shall we have another go at Weymouth tomorrow?' I asked George.

'Why not? We survived today. We'll probably survive tomorrow. It was a wild ride, and we're learning as we go.'

The 0855 shipping forecast on 30 July was for wind fresh NW to W, with hail and thunder. This seemed favourable provided that the wind was offshore as forecast. George bought some hot lunch to put in our thermoses. We read the Pilot, which said that the Anvil Point area could be 'exceptionally rough when a strong onshore wind blows against the spring ebb stream.' It seemed that the cause of this was a combination of shelving bottom, race and overfalls on the ebb stream, and the long fetch of a WSW wind, but principally the strength of the tidal streams, which were considerably stronger than stated in a spring tide ebb. We decided to try to press on through the main part of the race and continue to Weymouth if conditions were favourable, taking St Alban's Head about 1630.

I arrived at *Calypso* after a dash through a downpour and discovered that George had dropped my lunch thermos in his hurry to get oilskins on. I found him salvaging my eight sausages from the floorboards. Clearly he'd intended to offer them to me for lunch complete with slivers of glass.

'You can see the bigger chunks, and you can probably swallow the smaller ones,' he assured me.

'I would rather go hungry,' I replied.

The wind was very squally, but averaging SW 4, so George took *Calypso* out with the small jib and six rolls in the mainsail at 1115. A black thunderstorm hit us in Poole Harbour entrance. Then torrential rain which flattened the sea. Then a hailstorm which covered the boat with ice the size of marbles. Then the clear wind began to pick up; SW by W, force 5. This was bad news again, as the wind was coming off the Atlantic, not off the land. The forecast direction was wrong, as it had been the day before. By the time we reached Peverell Ledge, the sea seemed almost as bad as the day before, but we knew what to expect, and decided to keep luffing and pumping until through the tide race. A big wave hit us on our starboard bow and we dropped like a stone with a big crash into the trough, stopping dead. This was awful punishment for a small dinghy built of plywood.

Surfing out of control

There was virtually no shelter on the rugged Dorset coastline ahead – mostly cliffs. We got within two miles of St Alban's Head before deciding to turn back and head east for the Solent: the waves were no longer so dangerous, but very large (I guessed 50–80 yards between crests). A lot of water was breaking on board, and we could not sail like this much longer without disaster striking. George was steering, teeth gritted in iron concentration, eyes focused on the wave ahead. He was luffing each big one the best he could, but we had the board half up again, and were being slammed sideways.

We could not risk being at sea any more, but to run back to safety in the Solent, we'd first have to survive the Needles Channel. If we

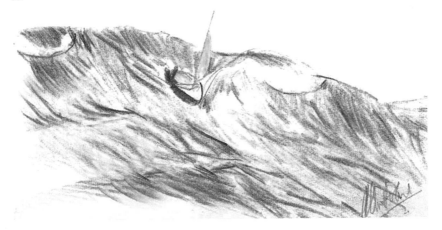

Surfing across Poole Bay.

arrived when the tide was ebbing, these big breakers would curl over and swamp us.

We had a wildly exhilarating ride for 20 minutes under reefed main alone. Our little dinghy was surfing like a speedboat, as fast as if we were water-skiing – probably 20 knots. A slight misjudgement, and we would be flipped over. It was both exhilarating and terrifying. There was a lot of weather helm, so we changed from the reefed main to the small jib at 1350 for safety's sake to reduce the strain on the rudder. Even so, we still surfed furiously under this tiny sail, with sheets of spray each side and a big rooster tail behind.

'When can we take the Needles?' I asked. They were 12 miles north-east of us.

'Not before low water at 1600, from what I remember.' We could be there within an hour. We had to slow down.

We could not check the Pilot with all this wind and spray flying. If we arrived early, it would have dangerous overfalls as the ebb tide ripped into the Atlantic rollers.

A little later I put up the genoa instead of the jib, since we could do with a little more sail area to keep control, especially as there was very little wind in the deep troughs between the wave crests. I was

Surfing at about 20 knots.

clipped on tight to the foredeck with my safety line. If either of us had been swept overboard, it would have been the end for both of us. It would have been impossible to retrieve the man overboard, and also impossible to sail singlehanded, as we needed both our body weights to keep the boat upright.

Broken rudder

At 1505, we decided to risk putting up the main and lowering the genoa. This was a big mistake. When we bore away, there was a loud crack astern.

'Rudder's gone!' I screamed at George.

Now we were in trouble, wallowing broadside on to the seas and risking being rolled. We had to get bow on. Fast. George streamed the drogue sea anchor from the bows and we pulled the rudder out and had a look. A quarter-inch bolt had sheared, causing the two arms of the rudder head to be bent outwards and split. We repaired it with long screws and a G-clamp as *Calypso* heaved and swayed in the big seas roaring by. I had fitted a long nylon warp rated at a one tonne breaking strain, and this allowed a lot of stretch so that the boat would not be tugged too violently as the big seas picked her up and flung her back.

We were off again on port tack under genoa, steering on the compass. The Isle of Wight was now five miles away, but frequently obscured by squalls and only visible from the top of a wave. At 1640 we saw a mast about two cables away so altered course and soon noticed it belonged to a large keelboat lying a-hull in the big seas. George streamed the drogue and we lay 50 yards to leeward of them to ask if they wanted assistance, but the roaring of the wind and waves made it impossible to communicate. They had broken a mainsheet block, and we waited near them until they gave us a thumbs-up. Later we saw them hoist a very deep-reefed mainsail and head for the Needles after us.

At the Needles Channel, the waves were breaking on the Shingles shallows to port, and smashing themselves on the white cliffs to starboard. We were committed – no way out of this. But as we got further in, the waves lessened until finally we were safe.

There were a few vicious patches of overfalls in the Needles Channel, but it was a huge relief to get back into sheltered waters again, between the Isle of Wight and Hampshire. We continued to Hamble and tied up at the yacht club. Wet clothing was stripped off and hung in the rigging. We'd taken big risks, learned a pile, and just about got away with it. But only just. A big sea could have flipped us. The rudder could have broken at a worse time, and caused *Calypso* to broach. We could have been rolled by the breakers. I never sailed an open boat is such dangerous waves again.

Sunday morning saw us buying stainless-steel bolts and screws to do a proper repair on the rudder. We planned to sail as far east as we could before nightfall – probably Littlehampton or Shoreham – so bought two more charts and set off with full sail up at 1105 in a westerly wind, just strong enough to plane. We put five rolls into the mainsail to lessen the strain on the rudder. At 1355 we gybed and broke the bottom mainsheet block, so came up into the wind, streamed the drogue, raised centreboard, lowered sails, removed rudder and examined the shattered block. We had no spares. We were able to effect a repair by boring a couple of holes, fitting on shackles and rigging the block upside down so that the damaged part carried one third of the strain previously on it. We also put three more rolls into the main for good measure.

George set about putting the rudder in. While I was hoisting the mainsail, the boom gave him a heavy blow on the head, knocking him out briefly. The rudder was floating away out of reach. After five minutes of efforts with sails, paddles and drogue line to recover it, we lost sight of it. George nearly jumped overboard to get it, but he was concussed, and could not have swum back to the boat. What to do now? We were off a lee shore with no rudder. How could we steer?

We had one course of action open to us – to make for Chichester Harbour under genoa, steering with the paddle pivoting in the hole under the mainsheet traveller. George helmed while I lashed the tiller to our other paddle to give us better steerage, and this proved much more manageable. We would need this on Chichester Bar, which we would reach at the worst possible time, about an hour and a half before low water. But at least the Isle of Wight should shelter the entrance from the swell, in which case it could be passable. For the next two hours we sailed on 85 degrees magnetic. Then at 1610 we lined up on the breakers we could see ahead, donned oilskins and lifelines, and stowed all loose gear. The bar bottom must have been very uneven, and we were able to avoid the worst breakers. The waves were big enough to give us some exciting surfing. We were in the entrance by 1630 – only just making way against the strong ebb stream – and reached up to Emsworth, scraping up the channel at low water, to anchor overnight. *Calypso* dragged her anchor and drifted away while we slept ashore, and was rescued by a fisherman. I paid him five shillings and thanked him profusely. That was as far as we got.

Interlude: ocean racing in two gales

In August, I crewed on an ocean race with a military crew skippered by an Army officer, to Spain and back, surviving two gales. We thrashed our way to Portland Bill, reefing down as the wind began to howl, and tacked. The boom was low due to the effect of the roller reefing, and smashed into the big brass compass, breaking it off its mounting. It crashed onto the lee scuppers and was on the point of going overboard. Bad news, as it was all we had to steer by. It was pitch black by now, and the seas were flying across the foredeck.

'Get the f.....g compass,' the skipper barked. I scrambled down and wrestled the big contraption back.

'Clutterbuck, get up to the bows and change the headsail,' was the next order. Two of us tackled the headsail as it was lowered to the deck, then clipped on the new one. Mountains of water cascaded over us. The boat dropped like a brick into each trough. I was violently seasick, but the waves washed everything clean.

I came off watch at 2200, and went below. I was exhausted, shaking with fear. The yacht had a steel hull, and the waves pounded into it like a steel drum. The noise was deafening. The skipper lay on the floor between the others, who were sandwiched and wedged in place either side. 'I knew you wouldn't make it,' he snarled at me. 'This is a tough business, not for a boy.'

I had to crawl to my bunk, which was the sail locker, being careful not to step on the captain. Inside the sail locker was a huge anchor, which bounced up and down, occasionally hitting the underside of the deck. If it landed on me, it would crush me. The only solution was to lie on top of it, and try to keep it down. Fortunately this torment did not last too long, as I was on watch again at 0330. We had a watch of two, a standby below of two for sail changes, and two off watch who must not be disturbed. These four below were often in a queue at the hatch to throw up over the side. All seven of us were seasick.

The gale subsided, but another was forecast as we entered the Bay of Biscay. I had no food or water for 36 hours. Rationing was imposed. Someone wrote in the log: 'Order of cannibalisation agreed. Target unaware, but agrees in principle.' The target was me.

There was another problem. We had 5,000 cigarettes and several crates of liquor, all duty-free and bonded, so we could not import these at any port. We had to consume them at sea. The crew had no problem disposing of the gin and whisky, but only one of them smoked. The only smoking I had done was a few puffs as a curious teenager, which labelled me as another smoker, and I was ordered to smoke 2,500 cigarettes in three weeks, which was 120 per day, or one every ten minutes while on deck. No one knew of the health risks then. I managed it by getting into the windiest places possible, and the wind did most of the smoking. I also smoked as many as possible in rough weather, so that the waves could extinguish them.

We arrived at Lequeitio in Spain, surrounded by village lights and steep deeply shadowed hills in the blackness of the night. There was a search party being organised, as we were two days behind the rest of the fleet. Next morning, the village was celebrating, with everyone dancing in the streets, blowing tin whistles and banging bongo drums. I had the pleasure of meeting two world-famous yachtsmen, both quiet and serious men. First there was Eric Tabarly, the French

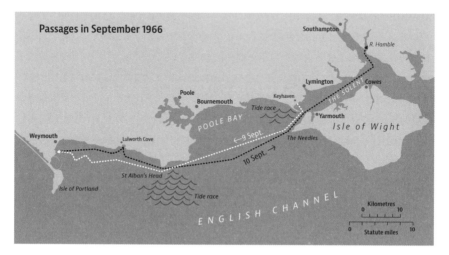

Passages in September 1966.

legend, winner of the 1964 Singlehanded Transatlantic Race, and then Adlard Coles, another remarkable legend. He was an enormously experienced offshore sailor, much of it ocean racing, and he had previously written a fantastic book called *Heavy Weather Sailing*, which was already the bible on the subject; he had also written the Pilot for the South Coast we used in *Calypso*.

Go west, young man

Back in England, I could go no further in *Calypso* until I had bought another rudder. I spent the next few days getting the boat ready, with a new rudder installed, and hitchhiking everywhere to get the next cruise organised. My uncle towed the boat to Keyhaven. George could not get away on the right dates, so I sailed with another friend, Johno Stokes. Johno was a powerfully built young man, full of confidence and a very experienced, unflappable dinghy sailor. I had total confidence in him.

Sinbad's hounds kindly broke into the clubhouse at Keyhaven on 9 September to wake us up after a night on the floor. We were off, headed west to St Alban's Head, which had already defeated me twice, and which we would have to take on the flood stream. We stayed close inshore and prepared for the worst of the tide rips. Ahead, a whole new series of headlands stretched out into the haze, and we had to continue sailing on a compass course. During my watch from 1905 to 2100 the wind fell calm, and I occupied myself after sunset by taking bearings on the three visible lights as night fell: Portland Bill, the Shambles and one of the Portland Harbour lights eight miles ahead. It was dark, and when I came off watch I decided to get some sleep so as to be alert when we hit landfall. I slept on the floorboards, jammed under the thwart. I woke up to find *Calypso* close-hauled a couple of miles off Weymouth. Soon we were both sitting out, and we arrived in Weymouth at midnight. The rest of the night was spent in a concrete bus shelter near the beach.

At 0650 I was woken by a deep growl and opened my eyes to see two black boots a few inches from my eyeballs. I looked up dark trousers and a dark jacket to a stern face six feet above. A policeman with a German shepherd was telling his hound to turf us out. This was too early for my liking but too late for the 0640 shipping forecast.

We left Weymouth and sailed fast on the plane with a following breeze, then stopped for lunch on the beach inside Lulworth Cove, which has a magnificent narrow entrance that is invisible from the sea. We planed in on a wave between the cliffs on each side, into a wonderful circular cove surrounded by steep crags.

On the way out of Lulworth Cove, the rudder downhaul snapped, and I quickly replaced it so as not to break the rudder and get wrecked on the rocks. It felt a little loose, so I tightened up the bolts underwater at 6 knots. We ran inside the overfalls at St Alban's Head, which were a mass of white water two cables to starboard – a dangerous place even for keelboats. Soon we were planing at 8 knots on big swells until we were stopped dead by equally big waves coming in

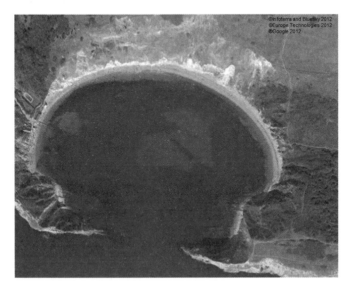

Lulworth Cove.

Johno Stokes in Lulworth Cove.

the opposite direction – an effect of the tide race. We went past the measured mile off Anvil Point at 8 knots. Johno was worried about a nasty brown squall cloud above us, which had several evil-looking tails hanging down.

As we planed up the Solent in the dark with spinnaker up, we lost the jib pole overboard, never to see it again. We arrived back at Hamble at 2300 after some hair-raising escapades with dense shipping. They could not see us, and we often had to alter course to avoid being run down. This trip had been successful. We'd had great weather, and we'd also done our first night passages, steering by the lights of buoys and lighthouses. There was a magic at night: bright stars and phosphorescence, the looms of distant lighthouses, the fear of not being able to see rocks or breakers, the need to feel where the ropes led to, and to know exactly where everything was in the boat.

What else could go wrong?

I joined the Dinghy Cruising Association and wrote an article in the autumn of 1966 on emergency tactics, feeling very honoured as a sixteen-year-old. Later in the year, I was asked to enter my logbook into the Wayfarer Class Owners' Association competition for the Viking Longship Trophy, which we won, much to my surprise.

I thought hard about what we would do if we were dismasted, drawing on my experience two years earlier on the Broads. We carried sheets of aluminium that we could screw around the mast. We also had plans to use wooden parts of the boat as splints. It was essential that some kind of repair was possible, as we had no means of propulsion other than sails. No motor, no oars, only paddles – which were next to useless at sea.

The next most serious breakage would be the rudder. This had broken already, and we had also lost it completely. We had put emergency repairs into practice, and had steered with the paddle. We were lucky that we were going downwind on these occasions, as this would never have worked with the stresses going upwind. One big problem was that the loads on the rudder at sea were huge

The Viking Longship Trophy.

compared to sheltered waters. We could see this from the amount of bend in the tiller shown in photos taken while we were running in heavy seas. The big waves were the cause, especially when we started to surf down the front face. At this point, the bows are dug in, and the undertow of the wave is bringing the bows rotating backwards to weather, while at the same time the stern is catching the crest and also twisting the boat in the same direction. If the boat heels, the problem is more intense, as the centre of effort of the mainsail is now no longer near the centre of water drag, and further twists the boat.

If not corrected by steering, or if overpowered, the result of this is a broach – a violent twisting of the boat to weather, ending up in a dangerous roll, beam on to big breaking waves. For our small dinghy, it would be curtains. We would be upside down in less than a second and unable to right the boat. To prevent this happening, the rudder had to be strong enough to manage the loads, which it was not. To compound the problem, the rudder of a Wayfarer is slightly raked back, rather than vertical, and this increases the loads. As it turned out, the rudder broke another eight times offshore running in big seas before we got the design modified. Each time this happened, there was a dangerous loss of control, and we were unable to sail on until either we repaired it, or we steered with a paddle or oar.

I thought about how to recover a man overboard, but realised this would be impossible in rough weather or at night. We sat only a foot above the water, and it would be easy to fall asleep and be swept off. Anyone falling overboard would have no chance of getting back to the boat, or of the boat getting back to him. We would have to keep ropes lashed around our chests at all times in rough weather or at night. Usually we did not wear lifejackets, reasoning that they would make no difference to our survival, only prolonging a lonely death.

I bought charts, and became engrossed in the lure of new harbours, tide races and overfalls, rocky lee shores, and adventures to new horizons. I read everything I could to learn how to fore-cast the weather from the clouds, how to survive disasters, how to sail in bad conditions. I plotted weather observations for the North

Atlantic in summer and was alarmed to see that a force 9-strong gale could occur every two weeks. These conditions would wipe us out, and we could not risk being at sea even in a force 7 or 8.

The lure of adventure in the world of storms and waves was irresistible. In the autumn, I set about investigating how to make *Calypso* more able to withstand big waves offshore. As chairman of the Engineering Society at my school, I was able to rent a film called *Summer Cruise*, the story of Frank Dye's 1964 sail in a Wayfarer from Scotland to Norway. He had been hit by a force 8–9 gale. He survived by lying to a sea anchor drogue with the mast lowered. The boat had been capsized many times by huge waves, and he and his companion had been flung into the water, weakening with each effort of righting the boat and bailing out the water. The mast was smashed to pieces. Their dogged determination to survive against all odds saved their lives, and they were able to jury rig and sail on to Norway. The film was an inspiration. It was watched by 133 of the boys, and I hoped it also inspired them.

I bought a book that had just been published called *A Fighting Chance*, John Ridgway and Chay Blyth's story of rowing the North Atlantic. They had had an epic struggle. They were both former paratroopers, and this tough background helped them survive. It was a heroic tale. George Greenwood met John Ridgway and was astounded to learn that they survived on 1,000 calories a day, which George described to me in a letter as a biological impossibility. I later met Chay Blyth, a Scotsman who looked indestructible.

To be able to sail in bad weather, we needed to be able to get water out of the boat fast. I installed a self-bailer. At high enough speeds, this would suck the water out, and reduce the need to pump continuously in heavy weather. I also made spray cover, about eighteen inches high, going across the back of the foredeck attached to the mast and shrouds. I made a template for this from brown paper and then sent it off to an outfit that made things out of PVC/nylon reinforced materials. That should reduce the amount of water pouring into the boat in heavy seas. It also had a top, which could be tied down on the windward side over the cockpit, protecting the off-watch crew member while asleep, or both sides could be tied to the boom in harbour for use as a temporary shelter. This was a revolutionary concept, and was to make offshore sailing much safer and more comfortable. It cost me £11. I got a radar reflector and waterproof navigation lights, which I would hoist up the mast to warn shipping. They were too dim to see more than a few yards away, but they made us legal.

In my school's engineering workshop I made a stainless steel cooker. It was designed to cook an army mess tin above a gas flame, with another mess tin on top keeping food warm. It was gas-powered, and installed out of the way, hanging in gimbals under the foredeck. I was hitchhiking to get all the new equipment between London, Cheltenham, Southampton and other places, often in my Army Corps military uniform, as many truck drivers only picked up soldiers.

I bought a one-piece oilskin so that I could sleep on the floor-boards under way without getting soaked. I tried it out by wearing my school uniform underneath it in a cold shower. It worked, and my jacket and tie were bone dry.

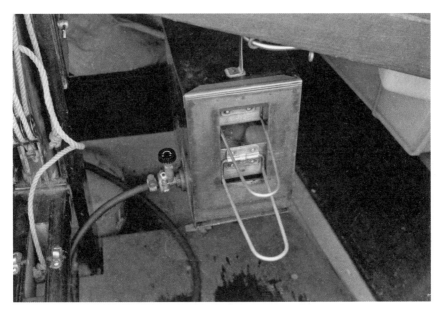

My cooker.

At the end of 1966 I left school and flew to Singapore, where my parents lived, and then on to Australia, where I worked my gap year before university, mostly as a labourer, and hitchhiking 9,000 miles after I lost my car in the middle of the Australian outback when it was written off with a blown-up engine.

In Sydney, I sailed with my uncle Bobby. He was a passionate sailor, and I enjoyed his company, talking about our interests in all things nautical. Bobby had been a submarine commander in the war, protecting the convoys in the North Atlantic, going up to Arctic Russia. He was also responsible for sinking enemy shipping, and had been awarded the DSO.

Francis Chichester had just arrived in Sydney on his quest to be the fastest singlehanded sailor around the world, and he was actually racing the times of the nineteenth-century clipper ships that went around the Horn a hundred years earlier. We saw him off on the second leg of his voyage to Cape Horn and England.

Bobby had a Sydney Harbour skiff, a hot racing machine that had a sliding seat which allowed the crew to sit way out from the hull. A cyclone (the Australian equivalent of a hurricane) came down while we were staying at Whale Beach, and I admired the power of the waves as they smoked in. After the storm subsided, a 'Southerly Buster' blew in. Bobby decided to take his other boat, a wooden Mirror dinghy, out for a sail, and he asked me to join him. We drove to the beach with the boat on the roof, and as soon as he'd undone the straps the wind blew it off, and it tumbled over and over in the sand. It was amazing that it was not destroyed. Not to be outdone, we went out anyway, Bobby skilfully steering the boat through big seas and stormy winds.

In July 1967 I hitched a lift with the Royal Air Force back from Australia to Singapore, and travelled on an Army ticket from there to the UK. Then George and I were off to Falmouth in Cornwall to launch *Calypso*. This time we intended to sail most of the length of the English Channel with the prevailing wind behind us. We would test our equipment and techniques in preparation for bigger challenges in years to come.

I got a waterproof radio direction finder (RDF) with money I'd made in Australia. This would give us approximate positions by homing in on radio transmitters when out of sight of land, and for listening to weather forecasts when the spray was flying. I also bought some oars. At 8 feet 9 inches, they were too long to stow, so I sawed them in half, and built a steel joint, so they could be stowed out of the way and then bolted together for rowing at sea. The blade half could double as a paddle. I also cut the tiller in two and hinged the two halves together, so that it could be swung up while sailing for access to the stern locker. For photographs, I made a box with a glass front, containing the camera wrapped in a plastic bag, and a remote release. In Australia I had obtained an aluminium space blanket, developed by NASA, and I got a zip sewn in. This would make it more comfortable to sleep at night, and would therefore enable us to do night passages.

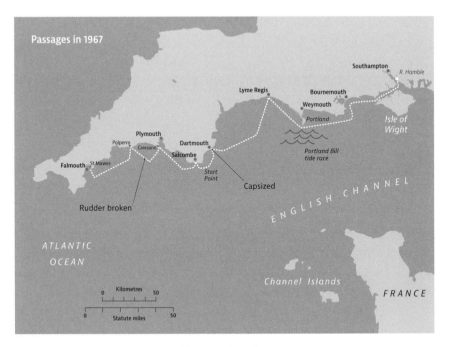

Passages in 1967.

Capsize

Our voyage that summer was more intelligently planned, as we could expect to be going downwind, with the westerlies behind us. We could not sail upwind at sea in anything much more than force 4, whereas we could go downwind in force 6, and possibly gale force 7, without taking our lives in our hands. We launched near Falmouth on 2 August 1967. The widest slipway in St Mawes gave us three inches to spare on either side of the Wayfarer's six-foot beam. We were both keen to be off as soon as possible, as we had both been working almost non-stop for the last 48 hours doing a year's worth of essential fitting out that had accumulated while I was working in Australia.

Next day, we left St Mawes in the midst of a squall with six rolls in the main, but the weather cleared quickly and we were soon running goose-winged under full sail in bright sunshine, George relaxing on the floorboards reading *The Times* in the shelter offered by our new PVC spray cover. It was so wonderful to be sailing on the open seas again.

We set a course of 60 degrees magnetic towards Polperro, racing a squall on the way. Six hours later, we rowed in through the very

Ready to leave Cornwall.

narrow entrance, the oars grazing the stone harbour walls, then left *Calypso* on a drying berth alongside the picturesque harbour wall with one boat roller as a fender and the other under her transom. We made a point of clearing the rocks from underneath her before her thin plywood bottom grounded. This was before the days of marinas.

On 4 August, the 0640 shipping forecast was 'Plymouth NW 4–6 gale 7 later with thunder.' Five miles north of the Eddystone Lighthouse, we needed to gybe, but the wind was too strong to do

A bird's-eye view of Polperro.

Rowing into Polperro harbour.

this safely, so we tacked through the wind. Ten minutes later, the helm went limp and *Calypso* spun round into the wind, twisting the rudder to an almost horizontal position in the process.

'Rudder's gone again,' I said.

What could we do now? We were a long way offshore, and would have to head downwind to hit land. We dropped the sails and put the drogue out. I had a look over the stern.

'The transom pintle's sheared off,' I told George. The top pair of rudder fittings was badly twisted. I put a bolt through the hole the pintle had left behind, as a substitute, but this too was unable to take the strain for long.

'I can't get a repair strong enough to take these loads downwind,' I told George.

'Then we'll have to try the oar, but the weather helm may be too much for it,' George suggested.

We tried an oar lashed under the mainsheet horse, and got under way under jib alone. We had a mackerel line, but had been unable to use it so far due to excessive speed. Now that we were under reduced sail, we put it out and soon pulled in a couple for supper, one before and one after a rather vicious squall.

We managed to balance the boat by moving our crew weight in, out, forwards and backwards so as to minimise the load on the steering oar. The Vikings must have known how to do this. When we hit land, we beached *Calypso* at the small village of Cawsand on a couple of boat rollers, then we fried the mackerel. I managed a temporary repair on the rudder pintle while we were high and dry on the beach.

There was a forecast of force 6 later the next day, and the weather chart in the newspapers showed a deep depression moving in from mid-Atlantic. We thought Salcombe would offer good protection from the weather. *Calypso* was high up the beach when we wanted to set off, resting on the two boat rollers lashed under her, so we rolled her 30 yards down the beach, George positioning our three boat rollers while I attempted to check her downhill progress by using the anchor as a plough – she weighed over a quarter of a tonne with all the cruising gear on board. This was a technique I imagined would have been used to build Stonehenge. No doubt the Vikings had also launched their longboats the same way.

Steady rain built up as we approached Salcombe and the wind came in short sharp gusts. We gybed at 1740 and George took her over the bar, goose-winged.

'Breakers ahead,' he said, looking on edge. The sea was breaking dangerously. We kept going and got through.

Our plan on this cruise was to make short daylight passages as far as Salcombe and then wait for 24 hours of clear weather in which to cross Lyme Bay, an offshore passage of some 70 sea miles, to Weymouth – the nearest port on the other side. It seemed unwise to attempt the controversial inshore passage around Portland Bill, as an inaccurate landfall could put us in the middle of the worst tide race on the south coast, potentially disastrous. The currents could exceed 7 knots, and could suck us into the race. Portland race is caused by very strong streams from both sides of the Bill, and its violence is increased by a shallow underwater ledge. It was the greatest challenge on our journey. In bad weather it would be worse than the St Alban's area. So we based our plans on keeping well offshore.

We left Salcombe in the late afternoon, planning our first overnight passage. The wind freshened and we had a good thrash to windward, reefing three times on the way until we had nine rolls in the mainsail. In the evening, we noticed a layer of cloud moving rapidly towards us from the west, causing a high sunset. It seemed to have suddenly sprung from nowhere and soon covered most of the sky.

'What do you make of the sky?' I asked George.

'Bad, very bad. It's warning us there's a gale on the way,' was George's view.

I agreed. We had to get to shelter, fast.

We would be safe if we could get into the narrow entrance to Dartmouth. But it would be dark, and there were high cliffs each side. It was exciting sailing as dusk descended. We were exercising

Rowing into Dartmouth.

the minimum control on the helm for fear of damaging our jury-rigged rudder pintle. We would have run the risk of broaching with the centreboard up in this sea, so had it three-quarters down. I remember asking George what he thought of our decision to call off the Lyme Bay crossing, and his reply was, 'There are too many fools on the ocean anyway – there's no need for us to be two more.' Nature's early warning system had impressed us both.

Conditions were far from ideal, as there was a heavy swell and it was a lee shore, so we took the normal precaution of assembling the oars in case of an emergency. We couldn't find the sector light and steered further to starboard, soon picking up a green fixed light which indicated that we were too far to port, close to large rocks. Continuing on starboard tack, we were getting very close to the rocks to the east of the approach when we suddenly noticed a red light: we had been looking at a green traffic light, and the real sector light had only just been turned on. We needed to gybe, but it was too risky, so we tacked around and sailed some distance before we were safe in the white sector. The swell was beginning to break as we passed the Castle Ledge buoy, and we soon doused the main as the wind became unpredictable under the cliffs. The sea began to break very heavily, and two crests broke over the stern.

Then, within a cable of the Castle, George started rowing, as we were no longer making progress against the ebb stream. However, we were through the narrows inside half an hour and went ashore for a much-needed pint in a pub at 2230. Back to the boat, and I took a spell at the oars as we went further upstream while George took over duties of navigator and cook. We picked up a mooring just before midnight, and after supper we kipped down with plastic bags over our sleeping bags to keep out the rain. We had no tent with us.

It blew hard and rained all night, and in the morning we ran under jib only in search of a better mooring. En route we heard the forecast: S/SE 6/7 going to E/SE gale 8 later. After I had been ashore to tell the Coastguard of our safe arrival in Dartmouth, we set off to beat back a few miles down the estuary with eight rolls in the mainsail and the small jib up. The wind was very gusty, funnelling upstream between the steep hills on either side.

I was at the helm at 1540 when an exceptionally heavy gust hit from abeam. Neither of us saw it coming, and the mast was in the water almost before we realised it. George was unfortunately caught the wrong side of the gunwale, trapped under the boat, and *Calypso* went 180 degrees upside down. We climbed on top to take stock of what was floating off, then righted her. I downed sails and started bailing while George swam around picking up gas cylinders, boots, oars, etc. Neither of us had lifelines or buoyancy aids on. I threw George's deflated Mae West lifejacket to him, and he was able to slip it on easily and pull the ripcord. The Mae West was a military lifejacket, used in Second World War aircraft and named after the Hollywood film star by aircraft pilots.

We finished bailing and assessed the damage. Lost overboard was the drogue, a box of emergency tools, the spare jibsheet, and the radar reflector. The stern locker and most of the Tupperware boxes were dry, but the bow locker was flooded. All our clothes were soaked. The RDF stowed in the cockpit was underwater for over two minutes but still worked, although at somewhat reduced power. It was ironic that we capsized in sheltered waters, but it further emphasised that we would be unlikely to be able to recover from a capsize in the open seas. We tried to blow our horn for assistance, but it was full of seaweed.

We tied up to a quay at Dartmouth. Occasion demanded that we break into our emergency rations and put a match to one of our cans of self-heating malted milk. This was basically a firework in a tube inside a soup can. Once lit, it burned and fizzed spectacularly. We stayed the night in the Boatel, using the boiler room for our clothes; our own room was soon an indescribable mess with electric razors, alarm clock and various other items being dried on our cooker, a dozen damp charts draped over furniture, and pound notes drying on the wall.

'We needed that,' said George, 'to improve our capsize skills.'

No land in sight and an overnight passage

Next morning saw us getting essential gear replacements.

'I'm not going without a radar reflector,' George insisted.

'That's mutiny,' I responded. I went to Salcombe to get one.

We left at 2230 on the Tuesday and rowed out into a dead calm in pitch black, but the swell was breaking in the approach and everything was thrashing around. The radar reflector came loose and crashed on deck. The wind picked up after midnight, and I came off watch at 0200. I put five rolls in the main before lying down to sleep on the floorboards, as the wind was rising. The spray was flying, and I tried to sleep inside my one-piece oilskins and waterproof blanket.

George woke me at 0500.

'There are two lighthouses out there – I think one is Berry Head and the other Start Point. Can you take bearings on them?'

Soon a faint pink light percolated through the mist. I tried to get an RDF fix, but could not hear the familiar Morse code beeps. It must have suffered a water leak after the capsize.

'We can't risk going for the Bill,' I said. 'We need the RDF to home in and avoid the Race.'

George was logical about it: 'Yes, and there's a mist. We could get lost. We've got to head for land.'

But where? The coast was almost devoid of good harbours. But there was one which we could try if the wind seas were not too big – Lyme Regis.

The sun broke through and the mist soon lifted. Our first dawn at sea. We stripped off our layers of damp night clothing and hung them in the rigging. We picked up the swell and planed hard and fast towards the land, supposedly ahead. This carried on for three hours.

'Where's the land?' I asked George.

'Don't see any.' George had the binoculars out. 'Just sea and a sharp horizon.'

And then, at 1020, 'Land-ho'. It was Golden Cape, visible now as it shrugged off a fog belt. There was a long south-west swell running, with waves rearing up above horizon level, and the thought of this turning into breakers near the Lyme Regis entrance worried me. However, it started breaking about two miles offshore, and the seas flattened as we closed land. We hauled out and left the boat on a borrowed trailer. It was time for George to leave. He had a busy schedule ahead, and I had to find another crew.

A sailing friend from Singapore was keen to join, but his father, a naval captain, forbade him to do any offshore passage in a dinghy. Colin Campbell – introduced to me via the Warsash Sailing Club – volunteered to crew.

I returned to Lyme Regis with Colin. In the harbour was a yacht bound for America which had just been dismasted in huge seas while rounding Portland Bill. We spent the night in *Calypso* on a boat trolley ashore. It rained steadily and we had neither air beds nor sleeping bags as all the gear was locked up with the harbour-master.

On 19 August we decided to launch, planning to take the inshore passage around the Bill at 1700. This would be safe provided we kept within a cable of the rocks. We aimed to close land three miles north of the Bill, catching the south-going eddy to the Bill and passing it just after slack water on the east-going stream, then using the north-going

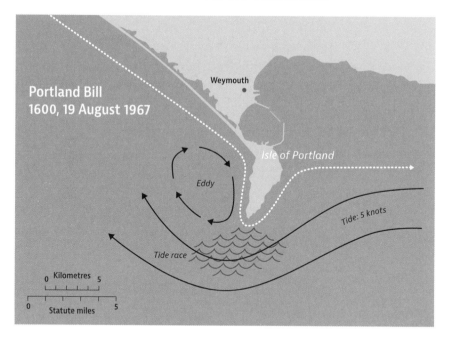

Portland Bill, 1600, 19 August 1967.

current to carry us away from the Race. I was very nervous about the Race as it was two days off springs and the tides could be up to 8 knots in a series of sets and eddies. Depths varied from 18 to 258 feet, causing havoc with the huge volumes of water flowing past.

Calypso was launched in the harbour entrance at low water, and we were off, working offshore before setting a course of 125 degrees towards Portland, which we could not see. There were numerous squalls coming off the land, and the 1355 forecast reported a shallow depression almost on top of us with a prospect of rain, fog and a backing wind. The weather was clearing, and we had the Bill in sight now. As we approached Portland, we focused on fixing our position to avoid being caught in an eddy which would take us into the Race. I came on watch at 1605, and Colin hauled in three mackerel before reefing in the freshening wind.

We were just off a rocky lee shore, and smashing into a choppy sea far too fast with a danger of breaking the mast. Further offshore to

Reefing off Portland Bill.

starboard, the sea really did look like the boiling cauldron Portland is notorious for. We passed the Bill at 1705, a few yards from the rocks in a much smoother patch of water. It was like running rapids in a big river. We worked northwards up the east side of Portland before setting a course for the offshore St Alban's passage, leaving the Shambles, another shallow area of breakers, to starboard.

We now needed to plot our course by dead reckoning, estimating our speed and direction. I got some practice estimating our speed by measuring the time it took for cork and sink on the end of 100 feet of kite line to run out.

Colin fried a mackerel in butter and lemon juice freshly squeezed from the citrus fruit we carried on board. I reefed down further as the wind was rising. After a red sunset, I fell asleep off watch on the floorboards.

I woke with a start as water was pouring over the side into the boat.

'What's happening?' I yelled at Colin.

'Not sure, I've lost my direction.'

The boom crashed over.

'Watch out!' Colin shouted. 'Wind's shifted. Gybing.'

Then everything was shaking. We were now tacking. Spray was flying. It was pandemonium. And it was pitch black – I could not

49

Colin Campbell at sunset.

see the ropes. Colin had lost his bearings. It was so close to being all over. Capsized in the dark, with me trapped under the thwart, and a long way from land. I would have been drowned, and Colin would have been in the water all night, or at best hanging onto the centre-board, likely to die from hypothermia before daybreak.

The wind had risen dangerously. We had well under half our normal sail area up, and both of us were on the gunwale, Colin sitting right out, racing style, with a jibsheet around his back, and even then we had to let the sheets fly in the gusts.

By midnight the wind had dropped enough for me to shake out five rolls, but *Calypso* lacked the punch to drive through the waves with this rig so I changed the jib for a genoa 20 minutes later. I wanted to get into Poole Bay before the tide started ripping westward at three knots, whisking us into the St Alban's overfalls. At 0100 Anvil Point was bearing 330 degrees.

At 0530, I took another bearing.

'What's the compass say?' asked Colin.

'330 degrees.'

'Then we haven't made any progress in over three hours.'

We had made hardly a yard of progress in the cold, wet, windy night. The wind was dead on the nose and we were continually trying to make enough of an easting to tack onto starboard and nip into Poole Bay without getting carried into the Anvil Point Race. I had nearly been wiped out there before, but this time it was dark as well. I crashed to get a few minutes' sleep. Three-quarters of an hour later Colin woke me, because the wind was up again and too much for him. Having crossed most of Poole Bay, we were now trying to get to the Needles at the western end of the Isle of Wight, but we could see nothing in the misty night.

I had intended to take the North Channel to avoid rough water at the Needles. The waves would be twice the size in the west-going ebb tide. By the time we reached Christchurch, there was a danger we would miss the tide through Hurst Castle. As the wind was offshore,

Beating to the Needles under the moon.

and it was high water, we cut across the Shingles, making use of the stronger north-east set. We were beating through Hurst Narrows and had 80 yards to go before clearing Hurst Castle when the tide turned. The approach of the ebb stream was marked by a line of smooth water coming from the north-east into the rougher water around us. We crossed back to the Isle of Wight and anchored, then we both slept in the sun until late afternoon.

We sailed the last few miles to Hamble, setting foot on terra firma at 2230 for the first time in 34 hours. This was the longest passage *Calypso* had yet made: 97 nautical miles.

3

Preparing for the Ocean

What had we learned?

The key lessons from this English Channel trip concerned techniques for sailing at night in an open boat. I was asked to write an article on the subject for the Dinghy Cruising Association magazine. Nearly 50 years later, I was surprised to come across it again on the internet. One of the attractions of night sailing was the sheer magic of sailing alone on watch under the stars, with the sea swooshing by, and blackness all around. Off watch on the floorboards, the stars twinkled above until sleep came with the constant noise of water rushing past just inches away. But it was also dangerous.

Everything had to be stowed away so that it could be found in pitch blackness. Tangles with ropes could be suicide. If there was an accident offshore, a rescue would not be likely. We had to avoid capsizing at all costs, all the time. A moment's inattention, and it would all be over. We learned to sail by the feel of the wind, as there was generally nothing to see ahead on the horizon to steer for. It was also imperative to keep warm, often from a thermos of hot drink.

It was easy to lose orientation, especially when exhausted from a sleepless night and intense concentration. An accidental gybe or tack could be fatal. Not releasing the mainsheet quickly enough could flip the boat in a second. Misjudging a wave was a risk, as we had to feel its shape and speed rather than see it, especially when running at night. We tried various watch systems: two on – two off, but this did not allow enough sleep; and four on – four off, but it was often impossible to stay awake for four hours. In later years, I found the best double-handed system to be simply to sail as long as possible, whether fifteen minutes or four hours, then wake the off-watch crew for a change.

Heavy weather required shorter watches. At night the on-watch person was sailing singlehanded, and the boat had to be rigged to allow all the sail controls to be reached from the helm position. The helmsman also needed to be able to navigate, with compass visible, charts in waterproof cases, and other gear accessible. We would use white painted areas on the deck to write on with waterproof Chinagraph pencils – bearings, estimates of speed and course, and so on. Man overboard could be avoided by keeping a lifeline attached at all times, even when asleep, so as to be ready for action in a second.

Hazards around us would be hard to see. We would rely on dead reckoning, assessing our speed and direction sailed since our last known position. We could use the RDF for approximate fixes, but these would often be ten miles off, and therefore not to be relied on for tricky landfalls. Shipping was unlikely to see our tiny light, or to look at the radar unless a light was visible, so we would have to avoid all ships. We quickly learned how to read their lights: masthead, port, starboard and stern. We often flashed a powerful waterproof signalling light directly at the ship, preferably using a Morse code signal letter. It probably made little difference, as the watch keepers only occasionally scanned the horizon looking for big ships. I remember a story of a ship coming in to harbour with a yacht's mast wrapped around its bow anchor. The crew had no idea that they had run it down.

There were advantages in sailing at night. The wind was usually steadier and less gusty, except in heavy weather. Great distances could be covered. Navigation was often easier due to lighthouses having a greater range of visibility than in the day, and each having a unique flash signature. Sailing by a full moon, with pupils dilated, would give enough light to read the chart by.

The sea takes no prisoners

Now we were ready to sail overseas to far-off lands. I got two labouring jobs to pay for the boat costs: one sweeping streets, and one on a farm lifting 90-pound wet straw bales with pitch forks. This built both muscle and money. George Greenwood had moved to Canada and was unable to sail again on *Calypso*. Then, in October 1967, I went to Cambridge University to read engineering, and also to plan the sailing. I came up with a scheme to cross the Channel and the Bay of Biscay the following summer, then go through the French canals to the Mediterranean. This seemed like a great adventure, and I spent long winter evenings planning it out.

At Cambridge I met Barry Hunt-Taylor (also known as BHT), who was interested in doing this journey with me. He was also studying engineering. He was strongly built, with a steady temperament and a great sense of humour. Barry and I became friends for over 40 years as a result of this. No one had ever done a cruise of this length before in a class dinghy. We would have to be much more self-reliant, and the boat would have to be much more reliable. We would be a long way from the coast, and unable to dash for shelter if the weather broke.

Much of this journey would be along the wild Atlantic coast of France, and we would need to be offshore, out of sight of land, much of the time. The North Atlantic had a fearsome reputation for storms. It had prevented Europeans from reaching America for centuries. Its westerly winds built big seas which dashed against the rocky west coasts of Europe. This would be more like ocean sailing than sea sailing. What challenges would it throw us?

I had crossed the Bay of Biscay before – but that was in a military troopship called the RMS *Carthage*. It was the winter of 1956, I was six years old, and my family had been posted to Malaya, where my father was to fight communist terrorists in the jungle. The ship had the remains of a gun turret on the bow. It had been fitted with eight six-inch and two three-inch guns for the war. A fearsome Atlantic storm hit us as we went south across the Bay of Biscay. Our cabin

RMS *Carthage*.

porthole was constantly battered. Everyone was sick. We had friends in lower deck levels who had to bolt down steel storm covers over their portholes. The waves were the height of the ship, rising up above the top deck 50 feet above the waterline. The waves were dark green, and white spray blew everywhere. The ship heaved, rolled and shuddered from end to end as it fought the storm. The waves broke the windows in the restaurant on the top deck, filled the large room and destroyed the furniture, which was smashed up as it surfed back and forth. The ship was 14,304 tonnes. Our Wayfarer was a quarter of a tonne.

I had learned from seeing rough weather that the sea takes no prisoners. On land, in a difficult situation, you can stop, or go back. On a mountain, you can go back down. You can go somewhere safe. At sea, everything is in motion – tides, waves, wind, storms – and you have no choice but to be carried along with it, adjusting to whatever nature throws at you. You cannot stop. You cannot just go where you want: not dead downwind due to the gybe risk, not into the wind, and in heavy weather you can only go on a broad reach. The sea anchor can help, but you are still carried by tides and drift, often in a direction you do not want to go.

I had also learned how helpful people are when they are absorbed in your project. Countless people helped us with the preparations and on the journeys, often because they were enthralled by what we were doing. Without much money, I could not insist on much, I could only ask for some help. Humanity was wonderful.

There were some challenges ahead. First, crossing the Channel, aiming to land on the Channel Islands. This would take over 24 hours, mostly out of sight of land, crossing the world's busiest shipping lanes – over 1,000 ships per day. We would have to cross the notorious Alderney tide race, which could reach some 10 knots. Exposed to an Atlantic swell, and surrounded by submerged rocks and ledges, this could be dangerous. But it was still safer than going west of Alderney, via the Swinge, which was even more exposed. The Channel Islands had some of the biggest tides in the world, up to 40 feet. They could rise up ten feet in an hour. Near Mont Saint Michel, the tide was reported to come in up the beach at the speed of a galloping horse.

Then we would negotiate the rocky coasts of Brittany, including two more tide races, Chenal du Four and Raz de Sein. Rocks apparently made washes like steamships as the water rushed past them. Without a motor, we would have to line up carefully in advance to get swept through without hitting rocks. Raz de Sein had been described as 'a boiling cauldron which belched and spat from the ocean floor'.

Then there would be a long crossing of the Bay of Biscay to Bordeaux. I read that sharks would investigate our small boat, and that the best defence was to ram an oar on the shark's nose. We would go through the canals to the Mediterranean – 300 miles of inland waterways. There were 153 locks on the canal ahead of us, and 245 bridges. It would be too long to row, but there was a towpath from the days when horses pulled the barges. We planned to convert one of us into a horse, while the other steered, in one-hour shifts. If we did ten miles a day, we'd cross the land within a month. We could expect temperatures over 40 degrees C. We would have to shut down in the heat of the day. I read that the lock-keepers would be cooperative if I gave them a cigarette, preferably English

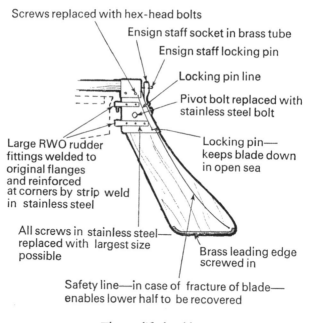

Screws replaced with hex-head bolts

Ensign staff socket in brass tube

Ensign staff locking pin

Locking pin line

Pivot bolt replaced with stainless steel bolt

Large RWO rudder fittings welded to original flanges and reinforced at corners by strip weld in stainless steel

Locking pin— keeps blade down in open sea

All screws in stainless steel— replaced with largest size possible

Brass leading edge screwed in

Safety line—in case of fracture of blade— enables lower half to be recovered

The modified rudder.

or American. In the Mediterranean, the Mistral wind funnelled down the Rhone valley, compressed by the Alps in the east to gale force or even storm force. Then I planned to get *Calypso* back on a French train.

I had to do something about the ongoing rudder breakages. Since the Wayfarer was a class design, it had to be built to fixed specifications. I wrote to Small Craft, who built *Calypso*, but they wrote a defensive letter back not wanting to supply a stronger rudder. I wrote to the designer, Ian Proctor. He thought the problems could be fixed by altering the sail trim.

Barry and I made new extra-strong fittings in stainless steel in the university workshops to replace the ones that came with the boat. We made a new oven from stainless steel, double-skinned for insulation and welded into a neat package. We planned to eat dehydrated curry and to load up enough for the entire cruise, about six weeks' worth. We would carry eighteen plastic water bottles full of either rice or tap water for ballast and cooking.

I desperately needed a place to rebuild *Calypso*. I had kept her at my grandparents' house, and as they had both been keen sailors, racing Y Class boats between the wars, they were happy to let me use a tiny wooden shed at the end of their garden. But it was not sealed from the elements, and I needed to strip all the paint off. My father leaned on an Army colleague to let me use a huge empty warehouse at 37 Corps Engineers Regiment at Liphook. A military forklift turned the boat upside down under a huge hot-air heater, and I stripped all the paint off, removing over 100 fittings, most of which were brass or bronze, and corroded in place. I dried the plywood hull for several days under a blower, making the boat much lighter. I painted the boat red so that it would be more visible, varnished the decks, and installed new, stronger stainless-steel fittings.

The Army compound was protected by guard dogs, and I was warned not to walk out of the warehouse at night. A burglar had recently scaled the double fence and been thoroughly mauled. The dogs were loose, without a guard, and were trained to latch onto

Preparing for the fit-out in an Army warehouse.

your arm with a permanent vice-grip and pin you down until the guards arrived in the morning.

One night, I was out too late, and noticed a dog loose. I held my breath and hoped it would not hear me or smell me. Fortunately it was upwind, and I crept back to the warehouse.

The sextant and the can of treacle

I taught myself astro-navigation. I bought a plastic sextant for £5, and the celestial sight reduction tables. I measured the vertical sextant angle of Winchester Cathedral, to assess its distance from me. I knew its height, so the angle enabled me to calculate its distance. This was an invaluable technique at sea, to measure the distance of a lighthouse, or a clifftop with a known height.

Next, I practised sun sights from the top of St Catherine's Hill, lining up the horizon, where I estimated the horizontal to be. This was not very accurate, as the horizon on land is not always horizontal, unlike at sea. To get round this, I opened a can of treacle, and measured the angle of the sun to its own reflection in the treacle, which was exactly double the angle between the sun and the horizontal.

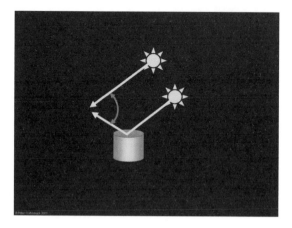

Reflections in a can of treacle.

The concept of astro-navigation is that the measurement of the sun's angle above the horizon, at a precisely known and accurately measured time of day, is compared to its predicted angle for an assumed location at that same time. The difference between the two enables you to determine the actual position relative to the assumed position along a line of the sun's direction over the water (the azimuth). This determination puts the measured position of the boat anywhere on a line at right angles to the azimuth. Since this does not fix the position, another sextant sight has to be done later, when the azimuth is different. So a morning shot and an afternoon shot are usually taken.

By estimating how far the boat has travelled in between these two times, the position can then be fixed at a point where the two lines cross. This technique only came about when John Harrison perfected a chronometer design in 1761. Before this, timekeeping was too inaccurate, because even a few seconds off could cause a navigation error of several miles. Harrison's chronometer enabled longitude to be determined accurately at sea, saving thousands of ships from wreckage, enabling the Navy to navigate the oceans with pinpoint accuracy, and pushing forward the boundaries of the British Empire. Before Harrison, astro-navigation could only

Practising with the sextant near Winchester.

estimate latitude, from measurement of the sun at noon, which did not require accurate time – although there was a highly complex method using sightings of the moon to determine longitude.

I tried this nightmare of 'sight reduction table' calculations. The technique was little changed over 200 years. I had to work out how far the point directly under the sun was to the east or west of our assumed location, known as the 'local hour angle', in degrees of longitude. I calculated this as 64 degrees. This required accurate time, as a second of error in the time would cause a mile of error in position calculation. The time was 1719 and 40 seconds. Additionally, the sextant measurement of the sun's altitude had to be accurate: a one-degree error in angle would be an error of about 60 miles in position.

I worked out the declination of the sun, in other words how far north of the equator it was: 9 degrees 57 minutes. This enabled me to know the point on the earth's surface that was directly under the sun, its geographical position. Then, from the tables, I worked out the azimuth, the direction of the sun's geographical position over the water, in degrees from due north: it was north 104 degrees west. More tables, and I got the angle that the sun should be at this assumed location at the time of the shot. It was 24 degrees 1 minute. After some corrections, the actual measurement was 23 degrees 50 minutes, a difference of 11 minutes. This put us 11 miles further towards the sun than our assumed position. It was magical.

I wondered how I could do it at sea, with the spray flying. Countless ships had been wrecked due to navigational error over the centuries. I glued some key pages from the Almanac Tables to a piece of ply and varnished them over so they were waterproof. Tidal streams were strong in the English Channel, and I practised plotting them from tidal charts. We were to have a major problem with this on our cruise. I got my wind-up analogue watch calibrated. Dozens of black and white Admiralty charts were ordered, to be kept in watertight plastic tubes in the bow locker. The charts in use would be folded around a ply board in a waterproof cover, for use in all conditions.

Several Admiralty Nautical Pilot books were bought. They could not be read in the spray of the cockpit, so we would memorise each section before leaving harbour. These were written over a century previously, mainly for the big clipper ships of the time. They had no photographs, and only a few drawings of coastlines for identification. Every page was full of dire warnings. It was gripping reading: even if a section of sea was free of the hazards of rocks and currents, then the Pilots were sure to warn of fog, or dangerous waves.

I tried a Pole Star shot, which allows a latitude estimate without accurate time, and it put us about 100 miles from where we were. I then did one on Jupiter, which was over 700 miles in error, due to a calculation blunder. I had to improve this reliability, as our lives could be in jeopardy if we got lost out of sight of land. I tried a selection of stars, and the moon.

I put in an advert for a crew in a yachting magazine, as Barry could only do the initial part, and George Greenwood was in Canada now, washing dishes at a ski resort to pay for his skiing. The crew had to have the right experience, and more importantly the right personality: tough, stable, dependable and with the right combination of courage and fear of the sea. Most of my sailing friends were teenagers, and their parents forbade them to do anything like this. My parents were against it, but did not forbid it, and I am eternally grateful to them for allowing me to do this wonderful adventure. They saw it as dangerous, but good for my development, rather like sending a soldier to the trenches.

I bought some seasickness pills and tried them out on land. They sent me to sleep for two hours, so were binned – this would have been a disaster at sea. I bought some self-heating soups with the internal firework, like the ones we used after our capsize the previous year. Also waterproof matches. We got a waterproof sleeping bag as well.

Making a dinghy into a home

We needed a better tent, and I made a wide roomy template in brown paper. It was to be held up by the boom and two halyards. It would be white, so that we could see well inside, and with big windows facing forward. This would only be used in harbour. I was concerned about our appearance ashore, especially if we were invited into a yacht club, and built a shelf in the bow locker for jackets and ties. I installed a pump on the stern bulkhead. I got a police firearms certificate so that I could buy distress flares.

The boom needed to be modified to prevent the aft end dropping when deep roller-reefed, and this was done by tapering the front and rounding the edges: also building a recessed, very strong, kicking-strap fitting. One issue was what do in very strong winds, when there would be too much for the mainsail to be raised. If we were running, we would be OK under just the jib. But if we needed to get off a lee shore by beating, we would need a trysail. I designed a 'trysail adaptor', which allowed the second jib to be set like a mainsail, from the mast luff groove. It was to save our lives on a dark stormy night as Atlantic rollers pounded onto a reef.

The tent, in brown paper.

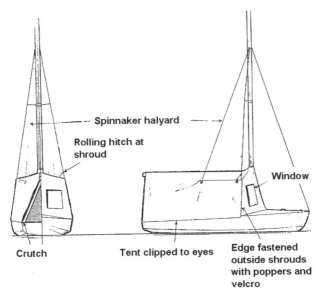

Spinnaker halyard

Rolling hitch at shroud

Window

Crutch

Tent clipped to eyes

Edge fastened outside shrouds with poppers and velcro

How the tent was fastened.

For extreme conditions, we would need 120 feet of warp for riding to the sea anchor, and Barry made a superb reel for this. Barry and I spent weeks in the barracks working on the hundreds of items on our list, to get the boat ready for the North Atlantic. Often we worked all through the night until dawn.

I was out of money for this extra gear, and rationed myself to avoid eating lunch, which freed up nearly a pound sterling a week. Later, I reduced my intake to six meals a week, less than one a day. This one meal was just cereal, and I had to give up two bits of bread for lunch due to shortage of cash. I was tempted to eat the treacle every time I practised the sextant shots. I started intense fitness training in my college bedroom.

All these preparations required travel back and forth across England, which I now did almost entirely by hitchhiking, always wearing my Army uniform. Before the days of fax and email, the only options for communication were mail or phone. I could not afford the phone, so everything was organised by mail.

Cooking curry in the cadet room.

We towed *Calypso* to the Hamble River and stayed in a yacht club cadet room, setting up our gas-burning oven on the carpet of this bedroom, and living off our dried curries. I hoped that this rather smart club would not kick us out.

My father was back from Singapore, and he joined us for a test sail in half a gale. This was to reassure Barry and him that we were ready for the Atlantic. Unfortunately a gust hit, and I was washed off *Calypso* while steering.

When I surfaced, the boat was capsizing, with Barry and my father being catapulted off. I had previously painted the bottom with a special black graphite paint, and this was very slippery. We could not right the boat, partly as the mast was in the mud 20 feet below. We eventually got back to the club, badly shaken. The issue of confidence was never discussed, however, and we went ahead with our plans in spite of this setback.

4

The Atlantic Coast to the Mediterranean

Across the English Channel

We were ready to cross the Channel on 24 June 1968, but several days of gales followed, and we moved *Calypso* into a derelict shed to finalise preparations. We stowed 35 plastic Tupperware boxes of spares, tools, food, equipment and provisions, mostly held in place by elastic shock cord under the decks. Then, after five days of waiting, we finally we got a good weather forecast.

We met Crab Searle. He seemed angry. 'You should not try to cross the Channel. Your boat is not suited to it.' I did not have the heart to tell him that was only 10% of the plan. The national *Sunday Mirror* newspaper interviewed Barry on the dock, and then we were off.

We beat towards the Spithead forts in the evening of 29 June as the sun went down. As darkness descended, we practiced reefing and being caught aback. We continued beating against a light south-easterly all night. When dawn came, visibility was poor and we soon lost sight of the English coast, to be left in our own world surrounded by a white-flecked blue sea. The wind was freshening. *Calypso* was soon quite a handful – doing six knots on a beam reach with the bows occasionally scooping up a foredeck full of water.

I was delighted to feel a tug on the mackerel line, as described by Barry in the log: '1400. Hauled in fish (mackerel?). Owing to

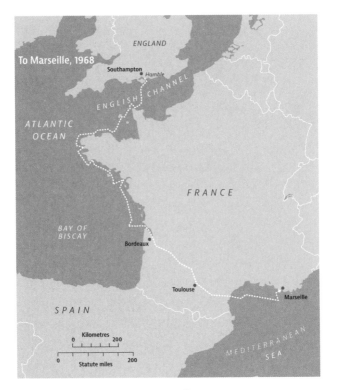

To Marseille, 1968.

inferior size of specimen, mercy and incompetence on behalf of the slaughterer, returned it to the sea.'

We had a dramatic experience with a tanker. It emerged out of the haze on a collision course and its portholes flashed past 20 yards in front of our bows. We were left tossing around in the wake, in the fine spray thrown up by the screw.

Calypso seemed in fine form, and not worried by more than her own weight of equipment and provisions. Somehow, a roomful of gear had fitted into two buoyancy lockers and 35 watertight plastic boxes. In a seagoing dinghy everything has to be watertight or water-resistant.

By 1545, I felt the urge to fix our position, as our dead reckoning (DR) now showed us to be nearer France than England. Barry obtained an excellent fix with the RDF, using St Catherine's and

Barfleur beacons, and the faint Morse beeps of Roches Douvres, some 150 miles away. I checked the radio fix by taking a sun shot with the sextant an hour later, and this tallied with our dead reckoning (DR) between the two. I was delighted that the complex process of celestial navigation was reliable. We worked out our DR using our estimated speed, calculated from the time it took for a float on 100 feet of line to pay out over the stern.

The 1758 BBC shipping forecast warned of extensive fog. We decided this was tolerable because of the number of radio beacons in the area, so set a course of 240 towards Cap de la Hague, hoping to arrive between 0100 and 0200 to catch the tide through Alderney Race and all the way to Guernsey. As we were expecting tidal streams of up to 6 knots through the race, I was anxious to get the tides right, so Barry and I did the calculations independently using different sets of tidal data, and we agreed on the result. I checked the time of my watch against the time signal from the BBC shipping forecast, as an error of a second translated to a mile error in the celestial fix.

When we picked out the French coastline at 2030 I felt much more at ease and expected an easy passage to Guernsey. However, we were

A near miss in the Channel (illustration by Gordon Horner for *Yachting World*).

to go through a set of alarming experiences in the next few hours. The sky clouded over before sunset and became grey and murky as the light faded – dramatised by lightning flashes and distant rolls of thunder, emphasising how exposed we were.

The wind was backing and increasing. We were approaching the race too fast and too soon. At 2300 we reefed down and reached north for half an hour while Barry fixed our position. By 2330 we were ten miles north-east of the race. I was very fatigued, and was hallucinating. I was sailing in zigzags, trying to avoid imagined fluorescent coils of barbed wire in the sea.

'Stop hallucinating,' I told myself. 'Don't fall asleep. Don't tack. Don't gybe.' We gybed and ran in towards the race against the last of the flood stream. The wind was round behind us and pushing us along fast, so that we were almost up to the race when Barry came on watch at 0030.

Breakers at dawn

I felt lousy when Barry woke me at 0430 to come on watch – shivering and stiff from cramp and cold. We were rolling round in a big oily swell with the gaunt shape of Cap de la Hague still on our port beam.

'Well, at least it's France,' Barry said, in an effort to raise morale.

'How was your watch?' I asked him.

'Fast sailing.'

The tide had been under us too.

'We should have covered twenty miles in the last three hours,' I said. I took a bearing on the lighthouse, and plotted it on the chart inside its waterproof case across my knees. We had only moved two miles, not twenty.

'I don't know what's happening. Maybe the tide was against us,' I said.

Barry was equally confused. 'The light has been the same direction even though we've gone miles through the water.'

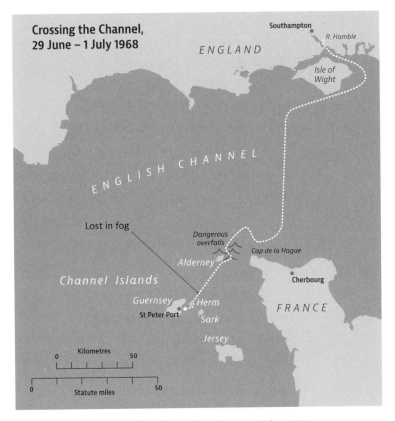

Crossing the Channel, 29 June – 1 July 1968.

We were learning that navigation was not an exact science, more of an estimate, or a matter of judgement. One bit of data often conflicted with another.

The sky at dawn looked ghastly – a tangle of red cirrus above us with several cumulonimbus clouds rapidly changing shape and blotting out the yellow sun, and a black horizon to windward. The ugly weather situation, and the strong tides, were giving me the feeling that we were in a trap. We were soon hit by a series of strong gusts coming from all round the compass and were forced to drop the main. The thunderstorms were coming at us. It was horrifying and threatening.

The sea was a strange sight – most of it smooth and glassy, but with areas of tidal whirlpools and overfalls, and occasionally darkened

Approaching France (illustration by Gordon Horner for *Yachting World*).

by a gust descending from nowhere – and the surface perpetually undulating as the big grey Atlantic swells marched in from the west. If the tide was running true to form then we had clearly missed it to Guernsey, so we decided to try to reach shelter in Alderney before the weather broke.

'I'll start rowing,' Barry said. 'This is not a good place to be.'

I was horrified to see in the distance a white wall of breakers, advancing rapidly across the sea towards us. What was this?

'What's happening?' I asked Barry.

'There's a wall of white water coming at us. No idea why. We'd better be ready for it.'

I suddenly realised that the breakers were stationary, and we were being swept onto them by the tide. The swell was meeting an underwater ledge extending off Alderney. What would happen?

'We're going to have to go the other way, or we'll be swept through the breakers,' I said.

It was touch and go. They were curling over and roaring. Barry's knuckles were white on the oars, and he pulled like he was training

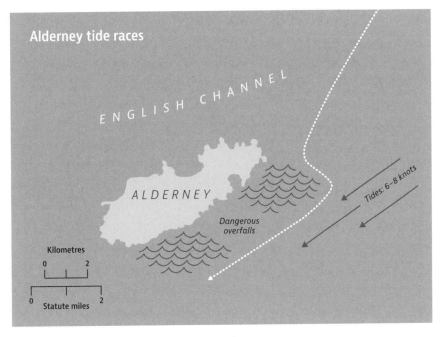

Alderney tide races.

for the Boat Race. I clutched the distress signals in one hand and the tiller in the other. Would we manage to make it round the breakers, or would we be drawn into the danger? Barry managed to pull hard enough to get to the edge of the worst breakers, and there were steep, dark waves ahead now. Our bows pointed up towards the sky and crashed down. A couple more, and we were through. I felt very frightened. We missed a disaster by a few yards. The roar of the sea reminded me that we were in a dangerous place. There was no wind, just breaking waves.

Soon afterwards the wind picked up and we were off across a choppy and confused sea, on a course of 240 degrees for Guernsey. Soon we saw an island coming out of the mist – identified as Guernsey from the Pilot diagrams but on a bearing of 215 degrees, so we altered course towards it. Twenty minutes later, another larger island emerged from the mist to the west of it – this one really was Guernsey, and on a bearing of 240 degrees. The mist and mirages had disguised Sark in such a way that it had resembled Guernsey in miniature. We had to reef at 1005 in the freshening wind – reluctantly, as we needed every knot to make way against the tide.

Barry soon identified what we assumed was Platte Fougère, a rock with two beacons on it marking the entrance to the Little Russel Channel, and we went up what we thought was the channel, only to find that we were sailing fast over unmarked submerged rocks. I expected to hit one any second. But we sailed on, avoiding the rocks skidding below us by looking for the turbulence of the tidal stream around them, and avoiding those areas. There was an island ahead of us, where open water should have been. There were, unfortunately, two rocks, each with two beacons on, and we had plumped for the wrong one. We guessed that the island was Herm. More fog rolled up behind us, so we could not turn back – our escape route was closed off.

Calypso was sailing fast but only just gaining on the increasing tide (we were later told that it runs at over 6 knots through the rocks).

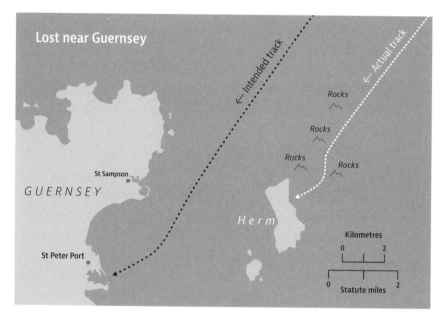

Lost near Guernsey.

We were in great need of a rest, so decided to land on Herm to wait for the tide to change.

We beached at 1130 and pulled her up on boat rollers with help from a couple of sunbathers. It was turning out to be a hot day, and we must have looked an extraordinary sight staggering about in thick layers of night clothing, oilskins, lifejackets, lifelines and boots, and slurring our speech through fatigue, while the onlookers were wearing bikinis. Barry, still clad in full oilskins and boots, collapsed exhausted on the beach and I feared he might have been put off sailing for life. Hundreds of sandflies were eating him, but I could not wake him up. He woke up in the heat of the afternoon, surrounded by incredulous children. Neither of us had had more than three hours' sleep in the last two days. We had both suffered from hallucinations in the night watches and had had to keep going on caffeine pills the last few hours. We had been lucky not to gybe or capsize during hallucinations. We had been at sea for three days and two nights, with virtually no sleep.

Four hours later we were off again, rowing between the islands of Herm and Jethou on a hot sunny afternoon. Barry then sailed her through a shortcut over the rocks to the Little Russel while I stood

Arrival at Herm.

up on the bows giving hand signals. We sailed obliquely across the powerful southerly tide in the Little Russel, finally fetching up at St Peter Port and dropping anchor at 1830. A hot bath was in order. I passed out from the fatigue, and Barry woke me from the dead by pounding on the door, fearing I had drowned. We slept on the floorboards under the stars, until rain came down.

Onwards to France

We were gale-bound in St Peter Port for a day and a half, during which time we replaced a shroud and did some other minor repairs and maintenance in addition to the traditional process of stocking up with duty-free stores, this being a tricky operation as it involved ferrying them to *Calypso* in our one-man Japanese rubber dinghy. We hauled it up and down the ladder bolted to the 40-foot-high harbour wall. That evening I wrote in the log: 'Yesterday's voyage seems a dream, or rather a nightmare.' Our new lightweight nylon/PVC tent proved itself admirably in some powerful gusts and heavy rain, but it behaved as a sail and the boat was tacking back and forth across the harbour. I plotted a weather map from pressure measurements broadcast on the Shipping Forecast. The low was moving away from us.

The 1758 forecast was good, so we left at 1805 on 3 July bound for the Brittany coast. This passage went smoothly, as by now we were used to the routine of living on board a dinghy at sea. Four on, four off, eating when hungry and sleeping when time for it. Navigation was certainly the most challenging aspect of cruising in these waters, and was almost a full-time job because of the complexity of the tidal streams.

Barry was seasick but stuck to his watches. We picked up the French coast at Les Heaux after 22 hours at sea, fixing our position on the lighthouse with compass bearings and distance off with vertical sextant angle. We were now running up the coast in a freshening breeze, and soon the tiller began falling to bits, so we had to heave to while I lashed it up. The tiller had been badly damaged just before we left Hamble and needed constant repairs on the cruise. Our chosen port was Perros-Guirec, a small drying harbour at the end of a bay protected by Île Tomé. The problem was to locate Île Tomé amongst a host of visible islands, and I set about this by looking for an island that subtended a horizontal angle of 7 degrees using the sextant. The approach was fairly easy, and we ran up proudly flying ensign, Q and courtesy flags. Our first view of France at close quarters was very satisfying as the skies cleared and the sun broke through to light up the pink granite rocks and the white houses dotted at random around the countryside.

Barry went ashore to look for a hotel and customs, and returned with tales of a fantastic welcome at a local bar. After anchoring we changed into our shore-going clothes (jackets and ties) and went into the village to be driven in style to the hotel complete with a three-man motorbike escort. We were soon local news, and almost everyone we met had heard of *le petit bateau rouge*. Customs formalities were very amusing as Perros was so rarely visited by foreign vessels, being a drying harbour. The *Douanier* had to brush the cobwebs off his rubber stamp and look up instructions on how to fill in the forms.

Off watch, trying to sleep (illustration by Gordon Horner for *Yachting World*).

We spent the best part of three days at Perros relaxing and enjoying French food, wine and hospitality. Barry had to return home to start vacation training on 7 July. I was sorry he was leaving, as he had quickly become a competent and reliable crew. His fluency in French and easy-going temperament were both invaluable qualities. I had problems, with over 80 per cent of the voyage still to come and no crew. The advertisement I had placed several weeks earlier had brought no response, so I returned to England with Barry via rail and ferry in search of a volunteer crew, while *Calypso* lay dormant in a boatshed in Brittany.

I found seventeen volunteers, but most backed out when they found out what was involved. I recalled Sir Ernest Shackleton's advert for volunteers for the Antarctic: 'Men wanted: for hazardous journey … constant danger, safe return doubtful.' Only Peter Jesson agreed to come along. He was a 21-year-old history student with a cool head and a thirst for adventure. Peter's sailing experience was limited to cabin boats on the Norfolk Broads, but he was tough and resilient, and had proved this on outward bound expeditions.

We left Perros two days late because I was attacked by German Shepherd guard dogs in a warehouse, requiring medical treatment. One lunged for my throat while the other sank its teeth into my leg. Luckily, the owner heard all the commotion and rushed out to shut down the attack, saving me from a gruesome end. Once I had finished the hospital treatment, we were ready to go.

Everybody in Perros was once again very helpful. One yachtsman was very interested in *Calypso* – saying '*formidable*' at every piece of equipment he examined – and he gave us a bottle of brandy '*pour les nuits froides*'. We were more than grateful for this, and often remembered him on cold nights.

Wild rides through tide rips

We launched *Calypso* at 1115 on 2 August. Ahead of us lay over 300 miles of rugged, rock-strewn coastline. At the western extremity of

▲ George Greenwood lining up on a wave 15-20 feet high.

▼ Over 500 items which had to be stowed in the boat.

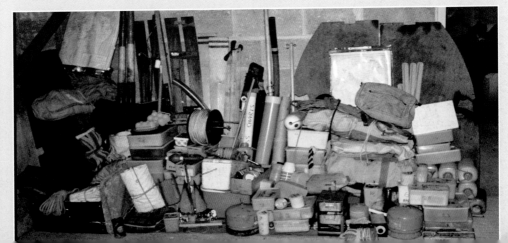

▲ Sorting *Calypso*'s gear: sails and sailing equipment, tent, food and camping gear.

▲ Gale-bound in St Peter Port, Guernsey, with our tent up.

▼ Peter Jesson keeping watch on passage in Atlantic waters.

▲ Clearing French customs at Perros-Guirec in Brittany.

▲ I take a sun shot with the sextant in the Atlantic.

▼ George Greenwood with the catch of the day.

▼ Peter Jesson plotting our position.

▲ One of the 153 locks.

▼ I am steering with an oar.

▲ Barry in the lock at Middleburg.

▼ Barry in *Calypso* at Amsterdam.

▲ Barry ready to launch *Calypso* down the shingle beach at Deal in Kent.

▼ A big liner coming out of the fog.

▼ Anchored at the uninhabited island of Ussholmen in Sweden.

▲ Apollo 11 landed on the moon while we were at Ussholmen.

▼ I slept on the rocks at Saltstraumen, Norway, where the tide reaches 22 knots.

▲ *Calypso* behind my Austin Healey 3000 on Mull, Scotland west coast.

▼ Tom off watch in the waterproof sleeping bag.

▼ Inside Fingal's Cave, Staffa, Scotland west coast.

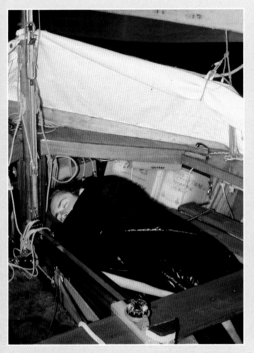

▲ My brother Julian at Fastnet Rock in 1993.

▼ Two men in a boat: Barry and I sail *Calypso* again after 44 years.

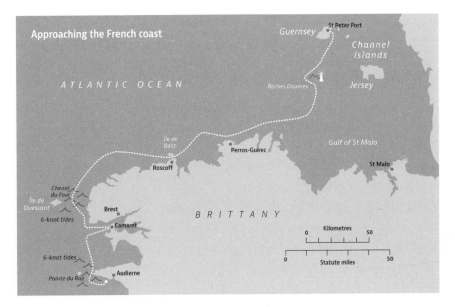

Approaching the French coast.

Brittany we would have to negotiate two tricky tidal races, Chenal du Four and Raz de Sein, where tidal streams run at over 6 knots and the rocks make washes like steamers. Then we had the south Brittany coast and a long stretch to the Gironde. And after that lay some 350 miles of inland waterways to the Mediterranean.

We worked our way down the rocky Brittany coast. I set the spinnaker and tried our trapeze, using an emergency shroud as trapeze wire and a safety harness as a trapeze harness. As a precaution I was tied to the end of 120 feet of anchor warp on a reel in case I fell off.

On the night watch, I kept falling asleep at the helm, which ran the risk of me falling overboard, or capsize. My eyes were glued to our small compass on a course of 250 degrees, and I was trying to keep our angle to the wind constant, feeling its direction all the time.

The dawn as we approached Chenal du Four came up cold and grey, with poor visibility again. The 0640 forecast warned of extensive fog in the rock-strewn race we were approaching. We were unable to see the coast – only the jagged teeth of off-lying rocks in

On the trapeze.

varying shades of grey. At 0920 the wind suddenly freshened from the north, and Peter reefed down the main. It was very choppy with a 3-knot weather tide.

By now we were poised on the brink of Chenal du Four, regularly and carefully fixing our position on Le Four lighthouse with compass and sextant. Soon we could identify rocks to port. The northern end of these was used as a landmark. More rocks emerged out of the mist straight ahead of us. The wind dropped to a calm, so we were carried through the Chenal by the tide, which turned fair. But with eight miles to go and the tide about to turn foul we were soon praying for wind. When it came, it freshened quickly from the NNE and *Calypso* was soon on a sizzling beam reach towards Camaret.

We spent a day in Camaret waiting for suitable weather to round Raz de Sein. Raz has a notorious reputation, and there is an old saying that '*Nul ne passe sans peur ou sans douleur*' (no one passes without fear or sorrow). It had been described as 'seas which rose straight up out of the ocean with the confliction of tide and currents.' We beat out of Camaret and through the Chenal de Toulinguet, which is bordered by Île de Toulinguet, completely pierced by a large hole. I was apprehensive about Raz de Sein, as we would be going through

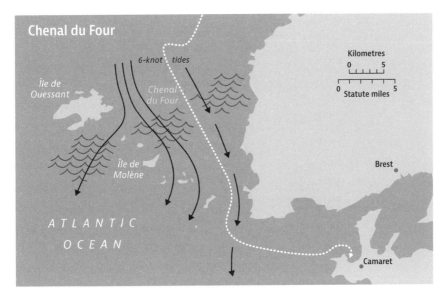

Chenal du Four.

on the full ebb stream, so we got our big pump set up and stowed everything away in preparation for a rough ride. This pump had a capacity of 18 gallons per minute, and swivelled on the stern locker bulkhead in such a way that it could be operated with one hand by the helmsman on the weather gunwale.

At 1745 I saw a section of coastline on our port beam. A lighthouse emerged from the haze dead ahead. It seemed so far offshore that it had to be Tévennec, so we altered course to go inside it.

Ten minutes later, Peter said, 'It looks just like La Vieille.'

It was La Vieille. We had been right past Tévennec Island, two miles to starboard, without seeing it in the mist. Right now we were being swept towards the dangerous white waters between La Vieille and Pointe du Raz. We hastily altered course and went through the race crabwise, nervously watching the frothing, turbulent seas on our port bow, like the rapids of a big river. We continued south through the swirling, choppy waters in the wake of the rocks for a quarter of an hour to keep clear of the northerly eddy in the steadily dying breeze.

Intended track

6-knot tide

Actual track

Crisis at Raz de Sein.

The sky looked very unsettled, and never had I longed for a thunderstorm so much, to give us some wind and speed. It was certainly preferable to the thought of being becalmed and swept through that maelstrom again when the tide turned in the night. Prayers were soon answered as a squall swept down on us and pushed us on to Audierne. We arrived there in the dark. Large crowds on the quay stared at us. We rowed up the river at low water past rows of ocean-going tunnymen looking very picturesque with their tall white-tipped rods illuminated by the quayside lights. We anchored over a spit so as to dry out and lessen the risk of being dragged under a bridge by the strong tide. There was only one other yacht on the river. I slumped back exhausted from nervous tension and woke an hour later to find that Peter had cooked up a steaming hot plate of prawn curry. The next morning, we were interrogated by the Directeur du Port, who thought we had yellow fever on board, due to our yellow Q flag (for quarantine).

We stayed in Audierne because of bad weather, but managed to leave on 8 August on a strong northerly, well reefed down. The passage ended with us beating up the well-lit waters of Anse de

Bénodet and anchoring just after midnight in the tree-lined Odet River, which is claimed to be the most beautiful in France.

Calypso normally attracted a lot of attention with her red ensign up, and much of our time would be spent answering a barrage of questions in French about the boat, our equipment, the weather we had had and other aspects of the voyage. One of the most frequent comments was '*Pas de cabine?*' accompanied by a typical French gesture of amazement. Throughout the cruise we found the locals very helpful and hospitable. Peter said he had never had so many free drinks in his life.

Deep blue rollers

The next passage took us to the Îles des Glénan – a group of small islands, rocks and shoals mostly uninhabited except by the pupils of the famous sailing school, the Centre Nautique des Glénans. The instructors and pupils lived in tents. *Calypso* was beached on Île de

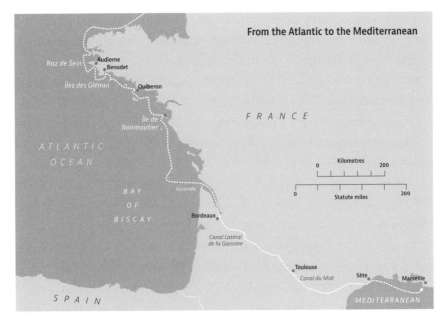

From the Atlantic to the Mediterranean.

Penfret behind a group of rocks which broke the swell, and energetically hauled up by the 'inhabitants', boat rollers being flung from stern to bow in rapid succession. After washing down a meal with their own homebrewed rough cider, we spent the evening singing around a log fire.

Saturday was spent exploring the islands. The Atlantic water was so clear that we never lost sight of the bottom. We left the flotilla with much cheering and waving, and after hearing the 1758 forecast (which as usual lowered morale – this time mentioning cyclonic winds, drizzle and fog) we passed the north end of Penfret and were on our way again. Distant thunder rolled across the ocean.

As the light faded in an ominous-looking sky, I went through the normal routine of preparing for night sailing: setting up the compass light, hauling our masthead light up on the burgee halyard and crawling into the bow locker to unstow air bed, plastic blanket and extra night clothing. Peter handed over as Île de Groix came abeam. My watch was spent avoiding steamers coming out of Lorient and trying desperately to keep awake – veering 40 degrees each side of our course of 135 degrees towards the Quiberon Peninsula still over the horizon. There was squally weather, with clouds scudding across the full moon.

I woke to the sound of thunderous surf. There was a big black rock behind the surf.

'What's happening?' I asked Peter.

'Big rock right next to us. Breakers and surf,' he replied. 'Do you know where we are?'

'There's not supposed to be rocks here. Must be off course.'

Peter bore away. Where were we? We avoided the surf and got away.

We spent four days gale-bound in Port Maria – days spent admiring the sea breaking on the rocks we had approached that dark night. This part of the coast is known as *La Côte Sauvage*, and justly so.

The excellent weather maps in *Le Figaro* gave us much to swear at. One night, *Calypso* had broken loose and drifted out to the harbour

Heading out into the Atlantic.

entrance. Peter had woken up, taken in the anchor, rowed back and re-anchored. This he told me as I gazed at the surf crashing on the rocks outside. I was more than grateful. But usually the anchor dug in firmly in the gales, and would not uproot even though *Calypso* tried to sail all over the harbour. She liked tacking into the wind, using the big nylon tent as a sail.

On 15 August we managed to sail round from Port Maria to Port Haliguen, a rough passage in the turbulent waters off the Quiberon Peninsula. This was the first we saw of the Atlantic seas which were to trouble us nearly all the way to Bordeaux. The waves kicked *Calypso* onto the plane, and she was often surfing along, throwing up sheets of spray from her bouncing bows. She was packed to the gunwales with equipment and provisions, so she did not lift onto the plane easily. The big waves helped.

When we arrived, we were dragged off to the yacht club, where the champagne flowed amongst much cheering and congratulations. We were later interviewed and photographed by the newspaper *Ouest France,* and they titled their story '*Deux jeunes Anglais sont venus de Southampton sur ce 5 metres.*'

Our friends in Quiberon wished us *bon voyage* and we set off on a fast broad reach. We passed Île de Houat and Île Hoedick with sails flogging in a squall and shortly afterwards had to reef as the wind came round on to the beam and freshened. The RDF was being temperamental and Peter could not pick up the 1355 forecast. All he heard was that there was a hurricane off Spain! This was disturbing, as there were a lot of cirrus streaks sweeping across the sky, heralding a depression. However, as long as we kept well offshore we were in no immediate danger. Visibility was excellent, and the land was below the horizon, so we were well off the dreaded Atlantic shore.

Soon there was a large swell running, very long but steep and breaking at the crests so that *Calypso* often had to be luffed into them. The spray cover really proved its worth, thwarting the progress of the heavier seas as they swept over the bows. The increasing swell worried us. It was a warning.

Nearly wrecked at night

We were about 20 miles off the French coast, getting ready for sailing on through the night. But something was ominous, not right. Peter was normally unflappable, but he looked worried.

He asked loudly, above the sound of the rising wind, 'What do you think's going to happen?'

'I don't know. There's a big swell running, so there must be bad weather coming at us.'

The sky was black to the west, and it looked like a huge, menacing squall. This had every aspect of the Atlantic in an ugly mood. The shipping forecast was imminent, so we hove to. I unstowed our waterproof RDF, which we also used for the weather forecasts, and tuned in. At 1758, the forecast started. But I could hear nothing except crackling noises. And then, when sea area Biscay came up, I could make out just one word, 'seven'. That meant a force 7 gale, way more than our little boat could survive.

I gave the RDF to Peter to re-stow, and set the boat back to sailing on a beam reach. The black sky was upon us. What was going to happen? White foam was being blown off the waves as the wind picked up to our weather side. Suddenly, it hit us like a rugby tackle. We were knocked down, and I let the sheets fly on both sails. The sails were flogging uncontrollably now, and shaking the boat violently. I could not luff up, as the wind was too strong. I dared not bear away, as we would take off like a rocket out of control. We could not stay as we were – we would be blown over, and we could never right the boat in such conditions. Night was coming, and if we capsized we would not survive.

'Down main!' I yelled.

The halyard had been carefully stowed so that it would run out with no delay. This precaution paid off. Peter got the sail down and into the boat in seconds. We now had just the jib up, but the rising wind still forced us over, with water washing into the boat. If the boat filled up, we would lose our stability and be rolled over. What to do now? We let the jibsheet fly, and it flogged ever more violently. It was too rough to risk going onto the foredeck to take it down. It was either going to shake the mast to pieces or tip us over. We were at the mercy of the sea. This time, it was merciful, and the wind dropped a little. Peter hauled the jibsheet in, and we sailed on. But the seas were getting rapidly bigger, and the wind was blowing the tops off the waves in sheets of white spume. The noise went to a high-pitched shriek. What options did we have?

Sailing on like this, with the waves on our beam, would be very dangerous after dark, as we would not be able to see them coming, and could be filled up or rolled over. Running for shelter was risky, as we would be surfing huge waves in the pitch black of a stormy night, and closing a lee shore without any shelter, and the risk of being wrecked on rocks or reefs. We could try to ride it out, lying to our small sea anchor, but this was also risky. If the weather got worse, the sea anchor would not save us. Also, we would drift onto the same lee shore about twelve hours later, without being able to choose which bit we wanted to be wrecked on. On this 100-mile stretch of coast, there was no shelter that we could reach.

'What do you think?' I yelled at Peter.

'We've got to get to shelter before it gets any worse,' he said.

'But there isn't any shelter,' I reminded both of us.

I looked at our chart inside its waterproof case. There was an island to our lee: Île de Noirmoutier. It had a bay on the side facing the mainland. But we would have to sail past the island, and past many rocks, before we could alter course for the bay. We would then have to beat into the gale to get into the shelter of the island. By then the waves would be huge, the night black. A Wayfarer could not beat into a force 7, even in flat water. In big seas, at night? We could never do it. I looked again to the west, where the Atlantic weather was coming from. The western horizon was still darkening and the rest of the sky becoming uglier every minute. We had to get out of this.

It would be dark by the time we were near Noirmoutier. The waters between the island and the mainland were strewn with rocks and reefs. But there was a lighthouse on the lee side of the island, and beyond this a beach. If we kept in the white sector, we would be clear of the rocks. We would have to head up hard on the wind and drive into this gale. We had never done anything like this before. If we could not, we would be smashed to small pieces on the reef in the dark. We would not be able to swim to land on such a stormy black night. We would probably not survive.

There was another problem. The boat would not beat with just the jib. To beat, we needed the mainsail. But we could not set the mainsail when the wind was this strong, even if we reefed it to a quarter of its size. I had made what I called a 'trysail adaptor' to cover such a situation – where we needed to beat, but could not set the mainsail. It allowed the jib to be hanked onto it, and then hoisted up the mast as a small mainsail, or trysail. But it had never been used. Would it work? Our lives would depend on it.

'We've got to get into the lee of Noirmoutier,' I shouted at Peter. 'That means the trysail adaptor. We've got to set it up. It's our only chance.'

We unstowed it and lined up the holes with the jib hanks, to make sure we could set it up while effectively blindfolded in the dark.

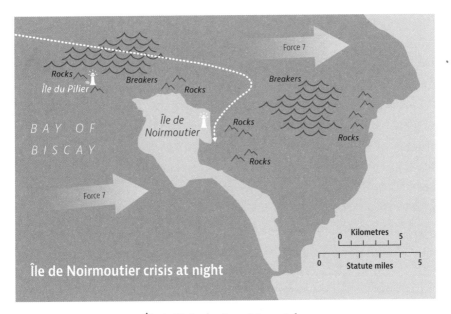

Île de Noirmoutier crisis at night.

So at 1850 we bore away and *Calypso* began surfing down the steepening waves in the fading light towards Île de Pilier, which guarded the north end of Noirmoutier. Soon we were surfing up waves as well. *Calypso* was in danger of driving her bows under, or being pooped by the large seas. The wind was rising inexorably. I was expecting the jib to be split in two any moment. The sky was black to windward, above us were red streaks of cirrus, and to the south it was a sickly green and yellow. Soon, some ragged brown clouds scudded low overhead and the rain began as the light faded. It was a frightening sky.

Calypso was planing continuously up and down waves like a speed-boat under only 46 square feet of canvas, and the safety line on the rudder blade was screaming. We could not risk going any closer to the rocks. We had to try to beat off them now. Everything depended on being able to sail to windward into the lee of the island. It was dark now. The sea was breaking around us on rocks and shallows. Ahead were more breakers. We had to turn and try to beat. Would the trysail adaptor work? Could we escape the rocks downwind of us? Could we control the boat on this stormy night? Would we be able to see the lighthouse and its white sector light? Could we point high enough to get to the beach? Would we capsize? Or hit a rock?

When we headed up, I was amazed to find *Calypso* would point towards the lighthouse, flashing at us through pelting rain. She was driving through sheets of spray in the howling wind, and the self-bailer was working overtime. The flashes of the light loomed higher and brighter in the rain, which was by now heavy and pelting horizontally. Soon we were round the back of it, where we found a mooring, got the tent up, unstowed sleeping bags and slept.

Three days and two nights at sea

Several violent squalls woke us in the night, and the next day it was still blowing hard, so we beached *Calypso* and relaxed on the island, sleeping on the beach. We launched early the next morning, and beat out in a stiff norwesterly with seven rolls in the mainsail. When the rocks to the north were clear, we bore away into

The self-steering gear.

an exciting broad reach, unreefing twice as the wind moderated. In the lee of Île d'Yeu we encountered some unpleasant seas as the swell came round each end of the island and pounded against each other. By evening, conditions were almost perfect – a good following breeze, a blue sky, out of sight of land in excellent visibility, and a deep blue swell so big that *Calypso* sometimes surfed down it faster than the wind, causing the sails to back. Almost trade-wind weather. We were even escorted by a school of dolphins, leaping together in time with the waves, criss-crossing just feet from the bows.

Peter woke me once in the night to say there was a ship on a collision course with us. It was extremely long, and festooned with white and red lights and far too close for comfort. My reaction was to flash our signalling lamp and jam my finger on the foghorn. Peter altered course by 80 degrees. The night was so black that we could not make out its silhouette. We concluded it must have been a tug towing a tanker.

I rigged up a system of ropes and shock cord on the tiller to get the dinghy to self-steer, with some success. At 1340, we did a radio fix as we had been out of sight of land for two days. We tacked onto 070 degrees towards the Gironde estuary. By now it was hot enough to sail in swimming trunks, 20 miles out in the Atlantic – one of the aims of the cruise had been fulfilled! I did the laundry by throwing it over the stern on a long line.

When we identified La Coubre lighthouse, marking the entrance to the Gironde, Bordeaux felt very close, though it was still over 90 miles away. We encountered a fleet of 40 fishing vessels. After the nerve-racking experience of weaving through them, we came upon hordes of jellyfish off the Royan Narrows just before sunset. They were so numerous and so large that a quarter of the water surface was covered with them.

Calypso was swept through two sets of overfalls in the narrows, and this was the worst we experienced of the Gironde's notorious entrance, where the big river flowed into the ocean.

The wind went round in the evening, so we were forced to beat up the estuary for the night and most of the next day. The night was brightened up by dozens of meteors flashing across the sky. Four on, four off, short-tacking singlehanded was tiring work. Then next morning the birds could be heard chirping in the trees as the wide estuary narrowed.

The wind dropped at midday. Rowing in this heat was no joke. We tied up at Bordeaux at sundown and stepped ashore for the first time in 60 hours. We had done three days and two nights non-stop. We were now surrounded by mosquitoes rather than spray.

153 locks

We woke at dawn, dripping with dew. It was foggy, close and very hot. The morning was spent removing mast, rigging and cover and reorganising the stowage layout, then we rowed off in the 4-knot fair tide through Bordeaux.

The Pont de Pierre was a hair-raising bridge. There were seventeen small arches in the strong current.

'Which one do I row for?' I asked Peter. He lined up on the middle one.

'Pull hard now,' he said, as *Calypso* was swept rapidly through the arch and into the vicious eddies the other side.

We continued rowing in half-hour watches, then were given a tow by a barge up the Garonne to the beginning of the canal at Castets. The tree-lined river gradually narrowed as we got further and further inland. We shared the first lock with the barge, then anchored stern to and kipped under the stars.

Up at 0630 and we rowed to the second lock, where our *Permis de Circulation* was examined and stamped for the first time. Peter towed *Calypso* to the third lock. We had previously looked on the canal trip as something of a challenge. We knew that there would be little barge traffic using the canal, so we were not relying on the chance of a tow. In the 1960s, there was also very little recreational

A double lock.

traffic on the canal. We had looked into second-hand outboards, and even small motorbikes to be used on the towpath, but we decided to rely on muscle power – towing and rowing. The worst situation would be manhauling – towing *Calypso* like a horse, using our safety harnesses worn backwards, and aiming to do two miles per hour for ten hours a day, which would enable us to cover fifteen miles a day, allowing for 20 minutes in each lock. At that rate, the whole distance to the Mediterranean would take us about a month, taking us into the autumn storms.

We were very lucky to meet a retired English lawyer, a Mr Roach, who was taking a motorboat to Majorca. 'Would you like a pluck? We're going all the way to Sète.' We were able to pull our weight by working the locks and helping with engine maintenance. Mr Roach insisted he could not feel us behind 256 horsepower, so we stayed with him nearly all the way to Sète.

The next seven days quickly developed into a routine. We would start off when the locks opened at 0630, hanging our sleeping bags and air beds over the mast to dry in the sun, as the dew was always heavy. From 0900 until 1800 it was very hot. It was hard work, leaping ashore, opening the sluices to empty the lock, opening the lock gates, hauling the boats into the lock and tying up the boats, closing the bottom gates and sluices, opening the top sluices and filling the lock, opening the top gates and then fending the boats off as they left the lock. A similar procedure in reverse covered the downhill sections. This was repeated 153 times. At night, we slept on the floorboards under the stars. One night, a rat jumped aboard to join us.

The canal as far as Toulouse is called the Canal Latéral de la Garonne, and it runs through pleasant agricultural scenery. The biggest highlight was crossing the Garonne river on a half-mile-long stone aqueduct high above the river at Agen. Toulouse was a well-laid-out city, shaded by rows of trees. Here we joined the Canal du Midi – one of the most outstanding engineering achievements I know. It was completed in 1681, after fourteen years of construction by an enterprise led by Pierre-Paul Riquet, to connect the Mediterranean to the Garonne River. Many of the locks are double, triple or quadruple, and at Fonserannes there is a staircase of seven. With the foothills of the Pyrenees to the south and the Massif Central to the north, the scenery is impressive. We went through a tunnel, 165 metres long, built in 1679.

Thunderstorms and mistrals

However, the nearer we got to the Med, the worse the weather became. On 27 August, the sun went behind a cloud for the first time in a week, and shortly afterwards a tropical thunderstorm burst upon us. The rest of the trip was completed in grey skies and steady drizzle. We spent the last two nights in the canal trying to sleep on the towpath under leaking bridges. We were through the 153rd and last lock by 0755 on the 29th, and after passing under our 245th bridge, we parted company with our tow and prepared for a sail across the Etang de Thau, a large saltwater lake.

This was very exciting, as we were surrounded by three thunderstorms. The wind was gusty and unpredictable. The mast was lowered again for the five bridges of Sète, and then we were in the yacht harbour, moored within 30 yards of the Mediterranean.

My image of the Med as a hot, stormless, tideless haven had been gradually shattered during the cruise by people who had sailed in it, and by study of the Admiralty Pilot. The weather was apparently unpredictable even by the French Meteo. The wind would either be above force 6 or flat calm, the seas were notoriously steep if it did blow, and there was perpetual swell even in calm weather. Marseille was no place for a yacht as it was crawling with Algerian thieves; the Gulf of Lyon between Sète and Marseille was the most notorious storm centre in the Med, and statistically we stood more than double the chance of meeting a force 8 there than anywhere in the Bay of Biscay or the Channel; the Mistral often blew at hurricane force and could last for 21 days; we had arrived at the worst possible time of year, and the summer so far had been the worst in living memory.

Some of this was told to us by a sailor who had been navigating on a yacht that had been wrecked two days earlier by a force 6 reversing its direction within two minutes. He also warned us of the mouth of the Rhône, which could be very turbulent, particularly after the recent heavy rain, and of how the Mistral funnelled down the Rhône valley and was very intense off the mouth.

We arrived in a forecast of force 9, and the swell was shooting spray 30 feet into the air outside the harbour. The next day the forecast was force 11, so we continued preparing *Calypso* for sea, and climbed the local mountain.

There was another *avis de tempête* (storm warning) on the 31st, but we were both fed up with waiting, so we left. I'd been told that

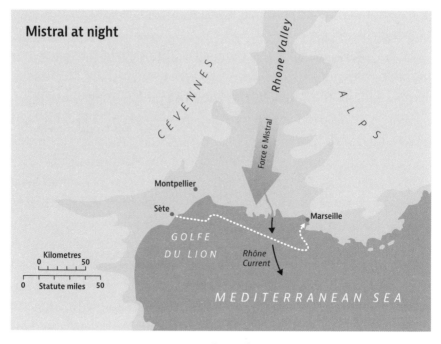

Mistral at night.

the fishing crews had rigged the forecasts so that they could have more days off work. The forecast was WNW 5–7 locally 9 off the Rhône. Everyone advised us not to leave, or to put into the harbour before night. However, I had a lot of confidence in the Wayfarer's ability to run before heavy weather. We started off reefed down in a fresh quartering breeze, then unreefed and had an exciting planing run.

Off Espiguette, we had to decide whether to put in to one of the ports to the north-west, or to continue through the night. There were no ports for the next 40 miles – to the north was the Camargue. The 1915 forecast was the same as before, and the sunset looked rather violent. But Peter and I were both keen to get this notorious stretch of water over with as soon as possible. We decided to continue.

That night I awoke from the port-side floorboards to find *Calypso* going very fast in sheets of phosphorescent spray. While flashing the signalling torch at a steamer, I noticed the water was brown. We

An exciting planing run (illustration by Gordon Horner for *Yachting World*).

were off the Rhône at last. Peter was doing a superb job handling her and seemed quite confident, but I did not like the thought of a capsize in the dark, so persuaded him to let me drop the reefed main. *Calypso* was planing so fast that luffing had to be done with the utmost care. We had to wait a couple of minutes before there was a suitably calm area to windward for the manoeuvre. Even under jib alone, she was soon planing wildly in the rising wind, shipping water above bow, stern and side decks: warm where it came in solid, but cold where driven into spray. Our powerful self-bailer was feeling exceptionally thirsty, sucking phosphorescent water out furiously – we could not have coped with this quantity of water by pumping. It was a force 7 gale. I focused intensely on our compass, lit by a dim, waterproof torch, keeping to a course of 70 degrees magnetic.

The dawn came up red, and silhouetted the mountains behind Marseille impressively. Suddenly we realised we had nearly sailed right past Marseille. We had somehow not seen the lights on the off-lying islands, and I had forgotten to allow for the Rhône current in our DR. Worse still, I had completely forgotten that there is a powerful current in the same direction if a Mistral blows.

Crewing for the America's Cup

We sailed into Marseille still under jib only for breakfast and had a week enjoying ourselves. I was told that the Mistral had reached gale force that night. We bumped into José Bacou in the street – we had known him before at Quiberon. He had heard when we arrived at Sète and had combed the coastline for us, thinking we must have put in somewhere because of the storm.

The Vieux Port is right in the town centre of Marseille and is used by pleasure and fishing vessels only. We later met the president of the Société Nautique and were made honorary members, so we could moor alongside the floating clubhouse. This was a hub of activity as it was organising the Semaine Nautique Internationale. *Calypso* attracted much attention and publicity, and one newspaper even said we had sailed all the way down specially to take part in the Semaine Nautique! Unfortunately the week was hampered by bad weather and Mistrals; broken masts were a common sight.

By this time we were very short of money, and our staple diet was bread, rice and watered-down wine. I was invited onto a Swedish yacht, and saw their Scandinavia charts, which started me thinking about sailing to Scandinavia the next year.

We met some very interesting people in Marseille – a Russian who had escaped from the Siberian salt mines on foot and lived in a mud shack on top of a cliff with no identity or means of income; Alain Gliksman, who led the Solo Transatlantic fleet much of the way until his rudder broke; an American photographer with the law after him; an English poet who had been round the Horn in a square-rigger; and David Thomas, who was skippering *Constellation* in the America's Cup trials. I was later lucky enough to have a place crewing on one of the Twelves – *Kurrewa V*, which had been modi-fied and renamed *Levrier des Mers*. I was stationed down below, on the big coffee-grinder winches below decks, working hard in a team of French gorillas, grinding in ropes which we could not see. This layout below decks was banned shortly afterwards. I was very impressed by the French challenge for the America's Cup – the young crew, who were mostly in the French Army, had a lot of team spirit and drive. David asked me to write an account of our trip for *Yachting World* magazine, of which he was Assistant Editor, and that helped cover some of the cost of the journey.

We did some cruising around the islands (mostly rowing in the calm conditions), and spent a night on a beach alongside *Calypso* at the end of Calanque de Sormiou, further east near Cassis. These calanques are like fjords but run parallel to the coast, so they are virtually invisible from seaward until one is almost in them. The coasts in this area we found very impressive, and the long journey to the Mediterranean had really been worthwhile. In sharp contrast to the commercial areas further east, there was not a sign of civilisation anywhere on the coast or on the islands. Just bare white rock and (in good weather) hot sun, deep blue skies, and of course no wind. The water was so clear that I could easily see our mackerel spinner hanging from its 68 feet of line beneath us.

On the south (seaward) side of a rocky islet we discovered white cliffs descending 600 feet into the sea. It was too deep to anchor, so one of us rowed while the other went over the side to snorkel under the cliffs. The view underwater was breathtaking. The cliffs

Snorkelling in the Mediterranean (illustration by Gordon Horner for *Yachting World*).

Calanque de Sormiou.

extended underwater as far as the eye could see. At one point, there was an immense submarine canyon so deep that the bottom was just dark blue in spite of the excellent visibility. I also enjoyed my first view of *Calypso*'s sleek black graphite bottom from underwater.

Peter left the next morning, allowing himself only three days to hitchhike to England. With his departure, I realised what an excellent crew he had been. It is a tribute to his equable temperament that in living together in a space just eight feet long and five feet wide, for six weeks, we never once had a serious argument.

Rough times in Marseille

I stayed in Marseille another month, looking for a ship to take *Calypso* back, and for work to pay for it. I wrote up the account for *Yachting World* while sitting in the sun in the boat. The article was entitled 'Away in a Wayfarer'. My photos were so bad that they commissioned an artist to paint what I had snapped.

When the last curry was finished, I lived on bread and water. I must have looked rather bedraggled, as I was arrested and locked in a police van for no apparent reason – I was later released back at *Calypso* when they saw the boat, and they apologised profusely. They had not believed my story until then. The dinghy was now my home in the Vieux Port, and the tent was up each night, as there were many downpours and thunderstorms. There were some disreputable people in Marseille, and I came across a group of destitute German youths who were living by selling their blood. I was also getting a bit scruffy, and my shirt had several rips in it, and had lost its buttons. I sewed it up, and also glued some of the other rips.

I found a ship that had just delivered a cargo of wool from New Zealand and was bound for England. On 23 September *Calypso* was

My home in Marseille.

Calypso being loaded onto the ship home.

plucked high in the sky by a dock crane and loaded on board, and shipped home for £25. She had been my home for three months.

I started hitchhiking back towards England, looking forward to sleeping in a real bed for the first time in two months. I travelled with an illiterate Arab convict on the run from North Africa, who had me in his car so that I could read the road signs. I got to Paris at the end of September, suffering from the cold nights as I had neither sleeping bag nor tent. I climbed the Eiffel Tower, as I had no money for the lift. By the time I got halfway, they had locked the gates going up further, and also locked the gates below me, trapping me halfway up the tower. I yelled for someone to unlock the gate. I nearly spent the night up there. My last few francs went to pay for the ferry back to UK.

I looked back on the voyage. The greatest problem had been navigation, often due to fatigue. *Calypso*'s great advantage over large boats was that she could be beached and anchored on drying berths – so we explored many areas inaccessible to keelboats. We had done some long passages, much of it at night.

This year we had not been plagued by gear breakages – mainly because we had time to stay in harbour in the worst weather, and also because of some 600 hours spent refitting before we set out. *Yachting World* also asked me to write up the refitting story as a technical piece, called 'Fit for sea'. As always in a small, open boat at sea, the crew is the weakest link. I was fortunate indeed in having both Barry and Peter. They were staunch and reliable. We also got along well, which is not always easy in a confined space.

I submitted the log for the Viking Longship Trophy, and we won it again. I had to make a speech in London when I was presented with it, which I was not very good at. I was now nineteen years old, but still short on presentation skills.

5

To the Land of the Vikings

Heading North

In the New Year of 1969, I ramped up planning for the next adventure. It started with a visit to the London Boat Show, where it was apparent that the Marseille voyage had generated a lot of good publicity for the Wayfarer class, in both newspapers and magazines. Peter Jesson had also been interviewed by the media. I spent some time on the Wayfarer stand, and was informed later that my voyages had caused a doubling of Wayfarer sales. In April, I received a letter from Tom Moore asking if he could crew for me. He had got in touch via *Yachting World*, having read the article.

I secured a major sponsorship from Vesta Curries. Six crates of them arrived at Cambridge railway station, and I took them to my digs in several loads on my motorbike. We would take all our food with us in the dinghy and eat curry at dawn, noon and dusk almost every day.

It would be another challenging trip, inspired by charts I'd been shown by a Scandinavian yachtsman in Marseille. First we would cross the North Sea to a European port, and sail through the Netherlands, partly 'inside' and partly 'outside', to the German coast, then to Hamburg and the Kiel Canal, and into the Baltic. We would then sail through the Danish islands, and along the west coast of Sweden up into Norway. This would be very demanding if there were heavy seas coming in from the Atlantic.

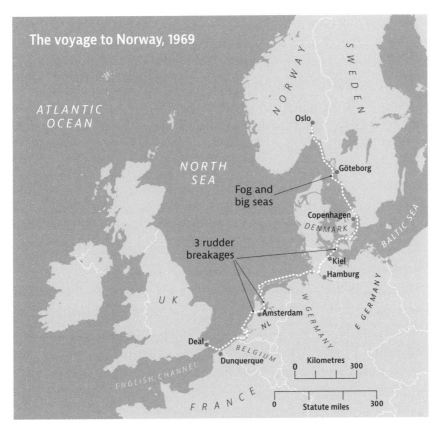

The voyage to Norway, 1969.

Barry Hunt-Taylor had recovered from the terrors of the Alderney Race and decided to do the North Sea section of our planned cruise. He had to start work on 7 July with BP in Hamburg, which is en route for Oslo, so the cruise offered him rather an interesting way of travelling to his job. Tom would join me for the second half of the voyage. We would have to push on fast, with little time to enjoy the places we stopped at, as I did not want to be at sea in the northern latitudes during the autumn. We could expect to be gale-bound for a few days en route, and we could not take any chances with the weather, so if I felt the outlook was risky, we would stay put. We had the treacherous North Sea to cross, with some overnight passages, and then thousands of rocky islands to sail through offshore Sweden.

We started from Deal in Kent on 21 June. Colonel Uniacke kindly let us use a Royal Marines warehouse for final preparations. *Calypso* lay poised on top of the steep shingle beach 20 feet above the surf. A couple of hard shoves and she was slithering down under her own weight into the breakers. A great way to start a long journey! We both jumped on board, then rowed off and hoisted sail, heading across the Straits of Dover on the first leg of the route to Norway.

The North Sea coast presented no problems beyond heavy shipping and shifting sandbanks. So we were off, *Calypso* carrying more than her own weight of equipment and provisions including seven courtesy flags, numerous dictionaries and phrase books, 34 charts rolled up in plastic tubes in the bows, and the stern locker half full of dehydrated food – mostly Vesta curries.

The English coastline gradually receded in British drizzle. We entered the shipping lanes, and we were soon becalmed for four hours in the middle of continuous lines of dual-carriageway shipping, rowing out of the way of oncoming ships.

By evening the sun was breaking through and we decided to head for the French coast to pick up the offshore night breeze, as it looked like being a clear, cold, starry night. By the time we picked up the lights of Dunkerque, conditions were so perfect that we abandoned our plan of visiting all seven countries en route, and decided to sail along the coast to a suitable port in the Netherlands. The wind had gone round to the sou'west and freshened enough to lift *Calypso* onto the plane on the steeper waves. The sky was crystal clear, with the red moon setting in the west, the Milky Way in a semicircle over the mast, and a lively phosphorescent wake. What more could we want? I spent the last of my watch steering on the Morning Star, Venus, rising in the east.

We changed watch again at that most miserable time of day, just after dawn. Barry struggled to get under the thwart into his berth on the floorboards.

'This boat is too small to fit in. Call this a holiday?' Then, mimicking a Cockney accent, 'Well, I dunno, I always does something like this in me two weeks off.'

A North Sea sunset.

Looking back to the previous year, rowing *Calypso* through heavy breakers at dawn in the Alderney Race, it seemed that he always did.

Inside Holland

Our arrival in the Netherlands was not as slick as I had planned. I leapt for the quay but didn't quite make it and fell in, while the yachting fraternity looked on. My jeans were brand new, so my underpants were pale blue for the rest of the trip.

The next day it was blowing hard, and there was a very violent thunderstorm. Our nylon/PVC tent dealt with almost all of the rain very well. The Dutch were rather horrified at our plans to sail up the North Sea coast of Holland, or 'outside' as they call it, and strongly recommended that we go 'inside' through the inland waterways, which they said were much more beautiful and less hazardous. So in the afternoon we reached across the Westerschelde in steady drizzle to Vlissingen.

We went through a lock with a trawler, tied to his stern. We had removed our rudder. When the gates opened, we were dragged out of control behind the trawler, and hit the wall with a crash. So much for the safety of the 'inside' route – *Calypso* had nearly been stove in and I'd nearly lost two fingers in a fairlead.

An hour later I was walking along the edge of the tree-lined canal towing *Calypso* to Middelburg on a calm sunlit evening. The swing bridge operators packed up at sunset, so we lowered the mast in Middelburg and sculled through this beautiful cathedral city. It was enchanting, with the lights of the city on either side of us.

Barry cooked a faultless Vesta curry, then towed *Calypso* to Veere, where we spent the night. At one stage, he was followed by an aggressive herd of cows. I offered to blast our foghorn but he said, 'For heaven's sake don't – they might mistake it for the mating call

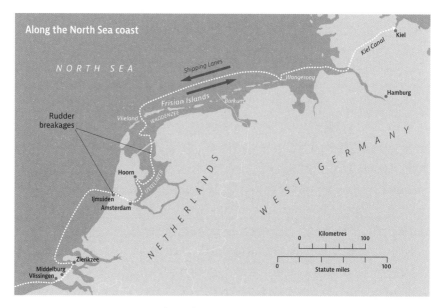

Along the North Sea coast.

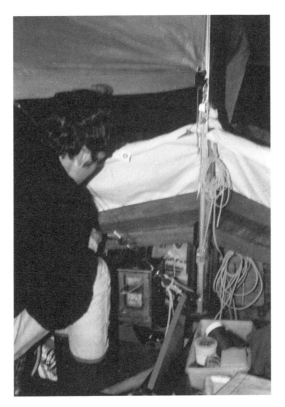

Barry cooking under way.

of a bull!' I decided not to aggravate the situation. We were hit by a phenomenal thunderstorm, and I had to sleep under a towel to soak up the drips from the tent. Three thunderbolts landed close by.

Another lock brought us to the tidal Oosterschelde, a big estuary, where we had a challenge navigating, as the only chart we had covering it was ten miles to the inch. The wind was fresh and we were planing hard, so we avoided white water indicating a sandbank.

I had plotted a weather map from the British coastal station pressure and weather reports; and as the situation looked rather ominous we decided to cancel the passage to Ijmuiden and put in to Zierikzee. This was a town out of a Van Gogh painting, with ancient lifting bridges, church towers, and windmills. As soon as we arrived, we were hailed by a Dutchman, Mr de Voss, who offered us the use of his yacht. He had read of *Calypso*'s cruise to Marseille in *Yachting World* magazine, and was extremely helpful. So we tied up alongside and moved in, and cooked and ate in comfort. On this voyage, we often found that people knew who we were before we got there, due to the publicity from our passages the year before, so we were hospitably welcomed.

We went off into town and found a small bar full of a rowdy crowd of the local young blood. Some visited our boat and one of them kept repeating 'I cannot believe it – such a liddle ship all the way from England.'

The next day we left for Ijmuiden, going 'outside' again, reefed down in a westerly force 5. We were beating down the Oosterschelde with inadequate charts. With the prospect of it freshening on a rather exposed lee shore, we decided to turn back. The run back to Zierikzee was very exciting, planing fast and overcanvassed, so we twice had the exhilarating experience of overtaking a wave – planing 'uphill', ploughing through the crest and surfing down its front face.

The next day, 25 June, we were able to leave, having had a lot of advice on the best way of getting safely out of the Oosterschelde. We beat out in the sunshine, and as the wind was light we chose the Krabbegat, which is the shortest but trickiest channel. The wind died and we ended up rowing, but the swell was breaking into surf to show us where the sandbanks were. The channel was not marked. There were breakers in every direction, all around the horizon. How would we get out of this? Then I noticed a tiny gap, which we shot through, with the seas curling over and breaking either side of us. We set our red spinnaker afterwards.

There was heavy shipping that night, and we used our signalling torch and foghorn a lot. It made no difference, the ships were unaware of our existence, and we had to get out of the way. Never mind our right of way as a sailing vessel – the ships were 50,000 times our displacement. I remembered a quote from my father – 'Here lies the body of Johnny O'Day, who died maintaining his right of way.

He was right, dead right, as he sailed along, but he's just as dead as if he'd been wrong.'

By midnight the wind had freshened further and we had the sea to ourselves. It was superb sailing, and I stood up by the mast for a few minutes just to absorb the beauty of it all. *Calypso* was planing most of the time, Barry helming her very skilfully, and it was such a warm night that we weren't wearing oilskins. The phosphorescence was everywhere in the fan of spray each side, in a deep jet coming off the rudder and on the crests of the steep North Sea waves. There is little to equal the sheer pleasure of planing in a dinghy on a night like this. But as the night wore on, I got desperately tired, and was fighting to stay awake. I focused on the compass lit by a tiny torch bulb. I knew that if I fell asleep, we would probably capsize and it would all be over. But we had to keep going to keep to our schedule, getting Barry to work in Hamburg in time, and reaching Norway before autumn.

By dawn it was rather different. Barry was dripping wet, thanks to a wave that had broken in over the quarter, filling half the boat. I had slept blissfully through it all in the waterproof sleeping bag, as the self-bailer sucked the water out.

I made a cup of coffee for Barry before he kipped down, and I was left with the problem of finding Ijmuiden in the poor visibility. There was no sign of land anywhere ahead of us, but it had to be there. The sun broke through for a few minutes, and a rainbow in the drizzle did a lot to uplift my morale. I sighted the skyline of Ijmuiden at 0530, and an hour later we were well inside the harbour. Then the rudder broke again at 0700. Barry steered *Calypso* with an oar through the smog of Ijmuiden, into the locks and thence the Noordzee Canal, while I did a temporary repair to the rudder.

We reached Amsterdam three hours later in grey skies and drizzle. On the outskirts of Amsterdam we were quite surprised to see a small, rather dilapidated ship with an enormous mast and 'Radio Caroline' painted on her sides – the most famous of the pirate radio stations. I had often listened to popular music from this ship. The government had banned private broadcasting in the UK, so the only way to hear new music was from overseas, such as a very weak signal from Radio Luxembourg, or from the stormy North Sea. Broadcasts were often interrupted by storms and DJ seasickness.

Soon the cold front came through and we were rowing around Amsterdam in search of a suitable mooring in half a gale.

'This is what I really like doing in my vacs,' said Barry, forcing a grin. Barry was a powerful oarsman, but the wind was often blowing us backwards. The water was very choppy because of the high concentration of barges, tugs, liners, ferries and so on all kicking up a wash and moving fast, trying to keep steerage way in the strong gusty wind.

We spent the best part of three days in Amsterdam. One evening we took the mast out of *Calypso* and rowed around the canals right into the heart of the city. Travelling around Amsterdam by rowing was really special. It was very pleasant and another way to enjoy this beautiful city, except that we got lost in the dark. Where we hoped to get out, we found the locks closed and locked. We eventually extricated ourselves from the maze, and after a lot of rowing we found another escape back to our moorings.

At 1415 on 29 June we left through more locks, safely under a bridge listed as lower than our masthead, then beating up the Ijsselmeer to the delightful little harbour of Hoorn. There were two bars in Hoorn, one where literally everyone was staggering around in an advanced state of inebriation, and the other almost deserted, with a prehistoric jukebox made from marble and brass.

We were sorry to leave Hoorn, another paradise with quaint old houses, 'Van Gogh'-type lifting bridges, windmills and thickly wooded shores all completely untouched by tourism. We broad-reached in the afternoon then had a hard, wet thrash to windward across the Ijsselmeer through the night. The rudder broke again at midnight. My repair had been inadequate and this time the damage was more extensive – screws and bolts twisted, a crack in the rudder head and three of the four stainless-steel pintle fittings damaged. What to do now? We still had around 1,000 miles to go, and the rudder was a major weakness. Steering with an oar was no problem and good for the biceps anyway, so we continued for our original destination of Terschelling. When we arrived at the locks at Kornwerderzand at 0200 the lockmaster told us that Terschelling harbour had been closed and Oost Vlieland was the best island to aim for. The lock was enormous, and we had it all to ourselves.

German sandbanks

Calypso was now in the Waddenzee at low water. A faint light signalled the welcome arrival of dawn. Our plans to take a shortcut across sandbanks were quickly altered when seagulls were seen walking around ahead. The water was only six inches deep! We had to beat round the seagulls' sandbank into the channel, which was marked by numerous buoys and sticks, each with a unique identifying feature, mostly bits of string and coloured rag – even a black bra on one of them.

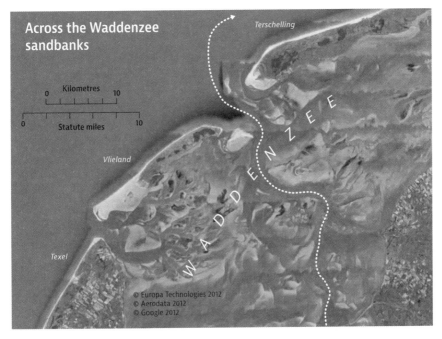

Across the Waddenzee sandbanks.

As the tide rose, we were able to cheat the foul stream and cut across the sandbanks, sailing in a foot of water most of the time. In these conditions an oar was just the job for steering. Vlieland, like the other Frisian Islands, is nothing more than a large sand dune, and when it emerged from the poor visibility we set about fixing our position on its lighthouse with compass and sextant to assess the tidal stream, as we had no tidal data for these waters.

The wind freshened as we approached the island, and I had great fun getting *Calypso* onto the plane again – but it was hard work with the oar. I found an ironmonger in the village who did an excellent job on our rudder fittings, repairing and reinforcing all of them for a small fee.

Next morning was glorious sailing weather. *Calypso* was planing on the steep seas. We passed a patch of shallows at 1555, taking one breaker unexpectedly aboard, then we were properly out at sea again.

We were out of sight of land now, and it was overcast. Fog was forecast. We had to get down to some serious navigation and settle into a four-on, four-off watch routine. We kept a navigational and meteorological record in all weathers, which was written with a Chinagraph pencil on white patches on the deck. This was used as a skeleton for our logbook, which was written up in fair weather or in port. In view of the poor visibility we decided to head offshore to buoy-hop down the middle of the shipping lanes, rather than risk being near sandbanks and shallows. We sailed along the shipping lanes through the night.

I heard Barry shouting through my sleep, 'Your watch now.'

I struggled to extricate myself from under the thwart. I could hear the rumble of a ship's propulsion coming through the water into our hull.

'Big ship out there.' Was it ten yards away, or a mile? I knew it could not see our small light on the burgee halyard, which would need to be a hundred times brighter to be visible. We had negligible radar signature. We had to be ready to alter course at any time, should a ship's bows suddenly appear.

'Can't see it, visibility too bad, no lights.' Barry was staring ahead. I shone a torch on the chart, where Barry had marked our last position. The ship's engines were getting quieter now.

'There should be a buoy five miles ahead.'

I swapped the tiller with Barry, and he got into the waterproof sleeping bag on the floorboards. I could not see anything through the murky blackness. I concentrated on the compass, lit by a battery light. We had to steer exactly 075 degrees to keep between the shipping lanes. I could hear another ship, but could not see it. After an hour, I steered with my foot so that I could plot our dead reckoning position on the chart. We should be at the buoy now, but there was no sign of its light in the misty darkness.

And so it went on through the night. With daylight came grey skies and drizzle, and very heavy shipping emerging from and disappearing into the mist, which limited visibility to a mile. The westbound shipping was passing a cable north of us, and the eastbound a cable

On the mud at Wangeroog.

south. It was rather like walking down the white line in fog on a busy main road.

By early next afternoon, the wind headed us and we decided to put into the German island of Wangeroog, which lay somewhere to the south of us. Soon land appeared, and Barry started unstowing the North Sea Pilot and other navigational gear, while I pored over the chart at the helm. The Pilot warned of unmarked sandbanks and tide rips. It seemed a lethal area.

An hour later, we were sailing against a 5-knot tide, with the heavy northerly swell breaking astern of us. Then we rowed round the back of the island, and jumped overboard in a frantic attempt to tow *Calypso* to the island before the tide dropped us on the mudflats. But we didn't quite make it. *Calypso* grounded when we were still about 200 yards from the island, and soon she was lying on a vast expanse of muddy sand extending about twelve miles to the mainland to the south. So ended our third passage of over 24 hours. Another 130 miles of fast, wet sailing.

I waded ashore while Barry slept on the nearest sand dune. 'What a way to arrive in Germany,' he commented. He wouldn't be leaving Germany for over two months, until the end of his summer job.

On the way back to *Calypso*, I got lost in the dark and had to home in on her while Barry signalled with torch and foghorn from the boat on the big mudflats. We were tired and demoralised, but the tides were such that we had to leave at 0300. Three hours' sleep would have to do.

When I woke for the 0202 shipping forecast the tide was roaring in at walking pace. Two hours later we were sailing through a violent tidal race in the approach, but the sun was up and soon we were sailing wearing shorts and enjoying a fresh following breeze. Morale rose rapidly.

The approach to the Elbe estuary was tricky, as the spring ebb tide was running hard against large seas, and these were confused further by very heavy shipping going to Hamburg. I was concentrating on avoiding shipping and gybing while *Calypso* planed goose-winged. In the middle of all this Barry was managing to cook scrambled eggs.

Barely legal in Kiel

We ran for another five hours up the Elbe estuary, partly under spinnaker, to Brunsbüttelkoog, where we locked into the Kiel Canal.

Yachts without motors were not allowed on the canal, so when I went up to the lockmaster to pay my dues, I was quite apprehensive. The lockmaster said, 'Ah, I see you have no motor, but I presume you have a tow with the other yacht on the lock,' to which I replied '*Jawohl*,' then went down the ladder, hoisted sail and we roared off in the fresh breeze, hotly pursued by an official launch. Five minutes later they had caught up with us, so we hoisted the ensign, smiled and waved. They smiled and waved back and passed us by. We were forgiven.

It was a perfect wind for sailing along the canal and we made excellent progress. It was also forbidden for pleasure craft to use the canal at night, but as we had not found a suitable mooring by dark we had no option but to row along, nervously keeping to the bank as the large vessels swept by, quite unaware of our existence.

It was another overcast day and we were glad to reach the end of the canal, where we shared the lock with nine ships of various sizes.

In the Kiel Canal.

117

An hour later we were tied up at the British Kiel Yacht Club, where we were overwhelmed by the hospitality of Major Shadbolt – the commanding officer of the Royal Engineer unit there. He and his wife took us into their own home. We had our clothes washed, and we had the luxury of a hot bath and a real bed again.

The next day Barry went off to start work at BP in Hamburg, where jaws dropped when he informed his employers of his chosen mode of transport. The orderly Germans could not quite understand how it had been possible to travel from England to Hamburg without showing a passport, or to get there by a 15-foot 'ship'.

I got a telegram from Tom Moore. He arrived next day by boat train from England. He seemed very keen, with a thoroughly professional approach to the whole business of dinghy cruising. He proved to be an outstanding sailor. He owned a Fireball dinghy, which he raced regularly, and he had done a fair amount of offshore cruising.

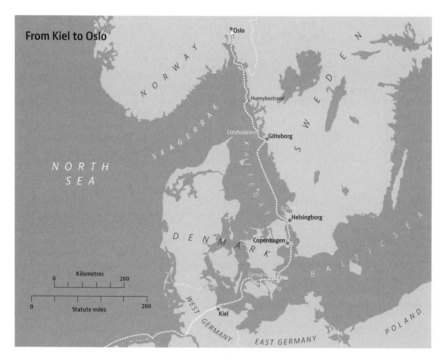

From Kiel to Oslo.

While we were staying with the Shadbolts we met David Houghton, the meteorologist famed for his work for the British team at the Olympic Games at Acapulco. He was also staying with the Shadbolts while reconnoitring the Kieler Bucht in preparation for the 1972 Olympics. His visit coincided with the arrival of a depression with winds forecast at force 9/10 for the area. So he was duly interrogated and asked why this sort of thing should happen in summer. I was fascinated to hear that it was of a similar type to the 1956 Channel Storm – the very rare case of explosive deepening of a wave low. However, this time it fizzled out.

Planing without a rudder

On the afternoon of 10 July we were off at 1520, sailing 50 miles across to the Danish islands. We were looking for a little harbour called Tårs Vig in the dark night. Suddenly we were surrounded by

Measuring our speed with a Pitot tube.

stakes, like being in the woods. Then we hit a beach. Where were we? We rowed off the beach and found the lights of the harbour at 0100.

Daylight brought a fresh norwesterly, and we were beating out of Tårs Vig with seven rolls in the main. We were on a very fast wet beam reach, with some exciting bursts of speed on the plane – too wet and violent to do any involved navigation, leaving a trail of foam ten yards wide.

Eventually we arrived at the island of Femø at dusk. I didn't think much of the leading lights, as the high one had been built in the middle of a forest and looked like anything from group occulting to quick flashing depending on how the trees swayed.

Soon the tent was up and we settled down for the night. The contrast between *Calypso* as a sailing boat and as a home never failed to surprise me. One moment the spray is flying and the off-watch crew member is huddled under the cover, and the next you are sitting on the same seat reading a novel by the light of the gas lamp with the sound of music and the smell of a meal being cooked.

The 0640 forecast talked about gale force 7 for German Bight so we stayed put and spent the day wandering around the island. The next morning we left, still in a nor'westerly air stream which was being sustained by a very intense anticyclone (1,037 mb) centred off Ushant. There was a very pronounced halo around the sun, warning of bad weather. We should have heeded the warning.

We sailed into the narrow channels marked by sticks and brushes. The scenery was beautiful – colourful undulating hills and rocky little islands – but we were not able to enjoy it for long as the wind freshened and we had to reef down.

At 1435 a gust caught us and the rudder broke for the third time. This time a reinforced stainless-steel gudgeon just snapped in two. Steering with the oar was something we were skilled at, so we decided to continue for our original destination – Copenhagen, by now 60 miles away.

When I came on watch at 1550, the wind freed, so we unreefed and had a tremendous sail, planing on a beam reach. It was shocking

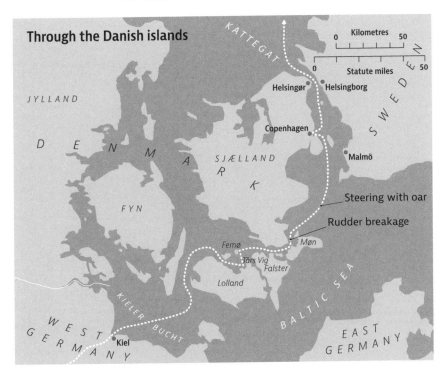

Through the Danish islands.

hard work on the oar. We were constantly adjusting sheets, sail area, centreboard, kicking strap and trim to balance the helm. When we arrived at the next headland, we found that *Calypso* had averaged nearly 7 knots. I thought it might be a speed record for steering with an oar in modern times. The Viking ships may have done better.

After this the wind headed us, and it was a long beat to Copenhagen, steadily reefing down as the wind rose. The trouble with steering with the oar was that the helmsman needed two hands for it, so the crew had to do everything else. There was no chance to get any sleep.

I did a radio fix as it got dark, then huddled under the spray cover to copy up the relevant information from the Pilot onto a waterproof pad.

I came on watch again just before midnight. I took over the oar. We were in a very dangerous situation: reefed down in pitch black with the wind rising, and no rudder. We had to get to shelter, fast. I

Tom steering with the oar in rough conditions.

was very scared. We had to focus intensely to avoid losing control of the boat and capsizing.

There was a loud blast right next to us.

'What's that?' I yelled above the howling wind.

'Huge ship,' Tom shouted. We looked astern to see a large tanker heading straight for us a hundred yards away. It had suddenly altered course. It could not possibly have seen us.

'Quick, flash the signalling torch. Blast the fog horn. Bear away.' Its bows were now above us, as black as the night, between its red and green navigation lights. We flashed our hand torches and bore away sharply. It taught us what a moment's inattention can lead to.

The shipping was now heavy, and as the wind freshened further we had to let the sails flog until there was a safe gap that would allow us to heave to and reef down again. Soon we had nine rolls in the main, which reduced it to about a third of its full area. Fifteen minutes later we were again overpowered, having to let the sheets fly. By now the wind was roaring in the rigging and *Calypso* was slamming into some steep seas – it was impossible to see them.

Copenhagen was now to the west of us, but our chart was far too small-scale to be any use and we could not read the Pilot in the driving spray. It was a hair-raising approach, with hydrofoils crossing our bows at 50 knots, not knowing we were there, numerous unidentifiable lights and unlit buoys.

'Can you see the harbour lights?' I asked Tom.

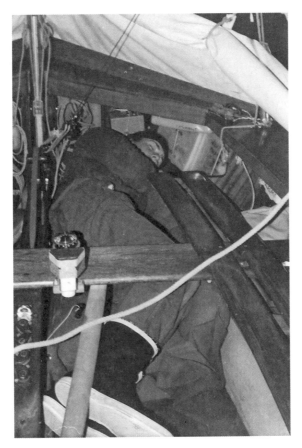

Off watch, under way.

'No, there are so many city lights.' Suddenly, I identified the harbour entrance lights. We were saved.

We tied up alongside an open whaleboat full of young Germans who invited us aboard for a drink, which tasted like neat alcohol. Tom went back to *Calypso* and slept soundly in his oilskins for nine hours, but I stayed on board talking in a mixture of English and German till dawn when one of the girls took me off to see the famous Little Mermaid statue.

We stayed in Copenhagen for two days while I got the rudder repaired. Fortunately I had a Danish dictionary, as small as I could get to save space in the boat. It was about an inch cube. The man who did the repair brazed the two halves of the fitting together and it got us all the way to Oslo.

Grete Nielsen, a journalist we'd met in Femø, said she wanted to write a story about us for the Danish newspaper *Aktuelt*, so she came down with a photographer and interviewed us just before we left. She wrote: 'Eyes are popping out when one is invited aboard *Calypso*. Other sailors in the harbour can tell *Aktuelt* that you have to know a lot about sailing and the sea to do such a trip. It's not written, but you have to know it all.' This was a big compliment from Viking stock. I was proud of my own Viking heritage, from the MacNeills of Barra, Outer Hebrides.

Thick fog at night

We decided to sail direct from Copenhagen to Göteborg so as to have more time in the islands further north. We spent all day beating up the Sound between Denmark and Sweden in a light northerly and hot sunshine. Then after sunset I went through the normal routine of preparing for a night's sailing: cooking a Vesta curry on our home-made gimballed oven; crawling into the bow locker to unstow the waterproof sleeping bag; unstowing extra clothing from the stern locker; assembling the compass light; hoisting the navigation light up on the burgee halyard; checking and replacing batteries or

The radar reflector.

bulbs on our pocket torches and the powerful signalling lamp; and, as the shipping was heavy, we decided to erect the radar reflector – a complicated operation involving five ropes and the spinnaker pole. We could see shipping altering course for us a couple of miles away as they picked us up on radar. In these waters, shipping was keeping a radar lookout, which usually they did not in the open ocean.

It was a calm night with light, fickle breezes. I came off watch at 0100, and Tom woke me for the 0202 forecast.

The next I knew, my feet were being kicked and shaken around and Tom was saying 'Come on, wake up. It's five o'clock.'

'What happens at five o'clock?'

'You know damn well what happens at five o'clock! I came on at one.'

'Oh!' More kicking and shaking brought me back to consciousness.

'It's five past five. It's your watch.'

'Oh, sorry.' I sat up and surveyed the scene around me. The sea was flat calm and full of jellyfish. There was thick fog and a ship was disappearing into it on our port quarter. There was a fog signal somewhere to starboard.

'I think we're about a mile south-west of Kullen.'

'Thanks, Tom! You should get your head down.'

We passed within a few hundred yards of Kullen but I never saw it, which was a pity as it is apparently an impressive headland. There were several ships sounding their foghorns. One dead ahead of us seemed to be getting slowly closer, and I was answering her blasts with our foghorn. She seemed to take ages to get any closer, and I woke Tom to help look for her. Then we could hear her engine-room telegraph. She must be just a few yards away, I thought. But where? The first we saw was the top of her bows. She was a big liner, doing about 1 knot. When she saw us, the engine started up and the bows had slid out of sight by the time the stern was in view. Neither of us had realised how thick the fog was – we had been expecting to see something near the horizon, not halfway up in the sky above us.

The next ship must have done a complete semicircle around us, judging by the blasts from her fog horn. I heard the bow wave before I saw it pass abeam of us – another liner. The value of the radar reflector was very well demonstrated, but I felt a bit guilty as the ships must have been as worried about us as we were about them, thinking we were big enough to be taken seriously. The fog had

Navigating with the RDF.

lifted by mid-morning but the shipping still altered course for us. The only one that didn't was a very rusty Russian trawler covered with radio masts and full of grimy-looking Soviets. It looked like a classic Cold War spy ship, and was probably reporting the ships going through the sound.

Visibility was still poor, so I did a radio fix on Kattegat South, Kullen and Anholt North light vessel, identifying their Morse code signals and then homing in. We needed to keep track of our dead reckoning position until we could do another fix. We had two ways of measuring our speed: one involved dropping a float on 100 feet of line and noting the time it took to run out, and the other was a Pitot tube held over the side.

In the afternoon the visibility suddenly improved, and about 20 miles of Swedish coastline was visible 12 miles to the east. The wind freshened during the evening and the sky clouded over. By the end of the day, *Calypso* was reefed down and planing on a broad reach.

In the evening I cooked up a curry. The North Sea water had been just right for curries. The Vestas we ate in the Baltic were short of salt, but they became steadily saltier as we went further north.

The rest of the passage was fairly rough and wet, but we were both used to our system whereby the on-watch crew member did all the sail trimming and navigation so that the off-watch man could get enough sleep. We were giving sleep maximum rather than minimum priority, and it made a tremendous difference to the ease with which we did a long passage. It was still a desperate struggle to keep awake steering on the long night watches, especially towards the end of the four hour stint, but it was better than previous nights when I often fell asleep at the helm, risking falling overboard or capsizing. A quote from the log captures the feel of navigating to a landfall at night:

2215. Picked up Fladden light four miles to west. Navigation wrong somewhere.

2230. Gybed onto port to reach Fladden Light through fishing fleet. Course 300°.

2320. Level w. Fladden Light within 10 yards to check name. Course 300. 6–7 knots.

2345. Hove to to check position and take caffeine tablets. Gybed back to 350° 0100.

0100. Wind S by E 5. Some heavy seas – careful steering necessary. Hint of dawn.

0145. TWM on watch with sore head – sat up too fast – hitting cooker eyelet.

0255. Level with Tistlana Light. Slightly too close in – danger of rocks.

0305. Gybed. Course 315°. Wind moderating slightly. Speed 5–6 knots goose-winged.

0320. Daylight.

0330. Hove to to fix position and eat so PRC could sleep on.

0440. Followed large German liner. PRC navigating. Narrow channel well marked.

0540. Tied up at yacht club after passage of 42 hours. Tidied up boat, then soup.

We were tired, having been at sea for three days and two nights. We were gale-bound in Göteborg for three days. Gale winds and rain battered our tent. Göteborg was a nice city, industrial, with a big port. We spent the time doing the host of odd maintenance and repair jobs that accumulate during a cruise. Gear on a cruising dinghy is subjected to arduous conditions – salt, sun, getting trodden on and tangled up in ropes, so it is essential to carry an extensive spares and repair kit. One of the beauties of a dinghy is its very simplicity – no winches, motors, lighting systems or other complex machinery to go wrong, but nevertheless we had had to make repairs to more than 20 items of gear. There was one job beyond our own facilities – making up and fitting a new burner for the oven, as the old one was badly corroded. For this, a Mr Johansson allowed us to use his metal workshop free of charge – a generous gesture typical of the hospitality we received. We had to start learning Swedish, and found that it was close enough to Danish that we could speak Danish and be understood. The newspapers reported the launch of the Saturn 5 taking Apollo 11 to the moon.

One night, I had great fun cooking a five-pan beef curry with rice, creamed potatoes and sliced runner beans, served with crispy noodles, raisins, chutney, sweet and sour sauce, followed by *café noir* and whisky as a nightcap. It tasted better than a five-star meal.

A moonscape as Apollo 11 lands on the moon

Finally, on 20 July, we left Göteborg and sailed some 30 miles north to an uninhabited island called Ussholmen. Navigation in these waters was demanding because of the number of rocks around. We

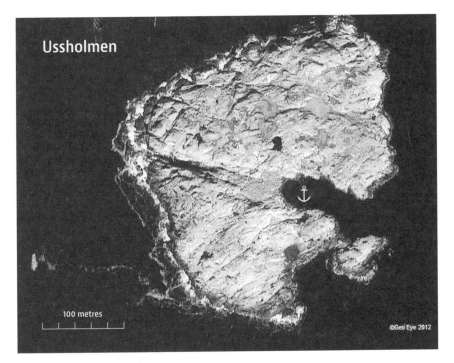

Ussholmen.

sailed well offshore, clear of the maze of islands. It was thrilling sailing – reefed in a fresh westerly and bright sunshine. The water was clear and reflected the deep blue sky. Big Atlantic swells were coming through the Skagerrak. There must be bad weather out there to the west. I looked at the chart, searching for an anchorage. There was a good one in a deep cove on the lee side of the island. When we got there, it exceeded expectations. The island was about 400 yards long, uninhabited, and completely deserted – just bare rock boulders, some moss, seagulls, and the sound of the waves breaking on the rocks to keep us company. There was no sign that anyone had ever been there. There were grooves in the granite where glaciers had ground their way across. It had an Arctic feel about it, in stark contrast to the woods and fields of Denmark. This was really what we had come to Sweden for. But we could not stay for long, because if the wind swung to the east, we would be trapped, and could be dashed against the rocks. We spent the night with our bows tied to those rocks, and our anchor out astern so as to keep us a safe distance from them.

It was in these surroundings that we listened to the first moon landing on the radio. It was easy to visualise the sense of desolation the astronauts must have had around them. The moon was shining on the granite around us as Neil Armstrong spoke from Apollo 11. It was a fantastic feat of technology and adventure, needing both brilliant organisation and plenty of good fortune.

Fog, high seas and big rocks

The next passage was the hardest *Calypso* ever did. It was blowing half a gale with fog. To avoid getting amongst the thousands of small islands and rocks, we decided to sail to seaward of all of them, and go from one to the next. But, like Apollo 11 we had to be exact in our navigation. Too far west, and we would not see the next island, lost in an area where we could not expect good RDF fixes. Too far east, and we would be amongst rocks and surf, unable to beat back out to sea in the big waves.

Bad conditions as we leave Ussholmen.

We would be sailing outside the main archipelago, picking up the westernmost islands, which were about eight miles apart. Visibility was such that we had to steer a course accurate to five degrees – almost impossible in heavy seas in a dinghy. We needed faultless teamwork between navigator and helmsman – the navigator to plot our DR course, and the helmsman to steer accurately, so that when all the tortuous sailing around big waves on the beam was averaged out, we had gone in exactly the right direction.

After breakfast I helped Tom get the tent down and stowed away, then scrambled over to the windward side of the island to look at the weather. When I returned, Tom was busy washing up.

'What does it look like?' he asked.

'Visibility is down to a couple of miles and the wind is freshening. We'll need a reef or two. Is there much left to do?'

'No. I've repaired the lilo and the bow locker is stowed away. I've been looking at the charts. Do you think we should set off?'

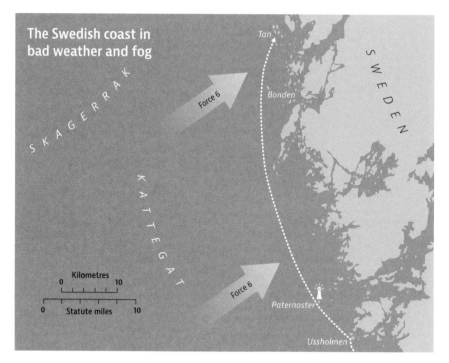

The Swedish coast in bad weather and fog.

'We'll be safe enough as long as we keep well offshore. Anyway, I'd like to show you what this boat is like in a sea. There's quite a swell outside.'

Tom was having another look at the chart.

'It's not the best place for the rudder to break again. There's rocks all over the place and precious few navigational aids.'

'The chart always makes it seem worse than it is. Anyway, I'd like to go. What do you reckon?'

'OK, Pete, let's go. I'll finish up this lot, and we could be off in half an hour.'

Soon we rowed out of our sheltered little cove, hoisted the main in the lee of the island, and put four rolls in. The reefing claw was clipped on, kicking strap tightened down, the hatches and rigging checked, and we were off. Soon the spray was flying. Tom, in his red oilskins and Mae West lifejacket, was busy checking over the

Tom reefing.

Tom using the sextant.

chart, which was now regularly sluiced with salt water. Beating out through a narrow gap between the rocks, a heavy breaker came on board, and we reefed again shortly afterwards.

It was a rare day of force 6 winds and fog occurring simultaneously. We rounded Paternoster, and at 1505 I asked Tom to take a bearing on the lighthouse before it disappeared in the poor visibility. It was the last landmark for the next ten miles, so I wanted a good fix as we were off a rock-strewn lee shore. He was soon busy unstowing the sextant in its Tupperware box under the foredeck and wedging himself in the driest place in *Calypso* – on the windward-side floor-boards by the centreboard case. It was virtually impossible, as the seas were too high and the lighthouse soon disappeared in the mist. Every now and then Tom would duck and protect the instrument as I shouted 'Watch it!' when a crest broke in. These were big seas from the Atlantic.

The wind was steadily freshening. An hour later we were planing most of the time. Grey skies, and large grey seas, but it was exciting sailing. From the log:

> 1615. Seas on the beam – much larger and some breaking heavily. Difficult steering as some need luffing, others bearing away to take astern – usually last-minute decision – heavy strain on rudder. Centreboard nearly up to allow her to slip sideways if hit beam on. Course must be within 10° to pick up island ahead – too far west and we miss it, too far east and we are on submerged rocks.

By 1630, Tom's DR estimate put us within expected sight of the island, but there was no sign of it. I was beginning to think that I could have steered a course inaccurate to at least 20 degrees. I was looking around for breakers but could see nothing except grey, heaving seas – breaking but definitely deep-water waves. There should have been a fog signal on the island, but we could hear nothing except the sound of the sea and the moan of the wind in the rigging. I thought I heard the sound of breakers, but could see nothing. I had two fears; first that we would not see any rocks, and be lost, with a risk of being wrecked later, especially after dark. Secondly, we might see the rocks but be unable to beat clear of them, and be smashed against them.

Suddenly we saw breakers close on the starboard. The whole island emerged from the fog. There were more breakers to starboard. Which island was this? What were these extra rocks. Now we could hear the fog signal: Tyfon and very loud. It was the right rock! The wind was still gradually rising, and visibility deteriorating, but there was a group of islands twelve miles ahead where the chart promised us shelter. From the log:

> 1715. Hove to. Put three more rolls in mainsail. Wind WSW 5–6. Planing hard on beam reach with seven rolls in mainsail. *Calypso* taking seas very well rolling if steep ones not luffed, but not dangerously. Some seas sweeping in over quarter. Self-bailer doing a grand job.

Tom came on watch at 1730, steering a course of 345 degrees, allowing seven degrees for leeway. He quickly picked up the feel of *Calypso* in these seas, and at 1757 feathered her along while I huddled under the spray cover for the shipping forecast.

Tom's helmsmanship was proven when Bonden Island emerged at exactly the time and place expected. I took a rough fix as we passed it, then we set a course for the next one.

Looking for islands.

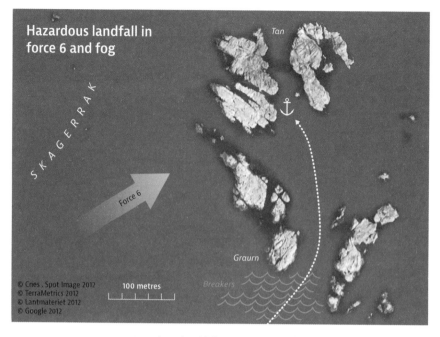

Hazardous landfall in Force 6 and fog.

We passed to windward of that one as well, watching the breakers shooting up the cliffs a cable to starboard. Tom was not in possession of the chart, and looked very worried, staring ahead intently when not lining up on a steep wave astern.

'There's another island dead ahead,' he said, 'and I think there's another one fine on the port bow – yes, there is – definitely. I can see the breakers.'

'That's right, Tom. There should be. It's all tying up,' I reassured him. 'We should be able to see a couple more in two or three minutes. We've got to take the gap between the two that are furthest to the right – it's fifteen fathoms deep but the other gaps are very shallow. We've got to get the right one. We won't be able to beat out in these seas. How's she handling?'

'OK, but I think they're getting bigger.'

'Probably shallower. The gap should be bearing about five degrees magnetic now.'

136

'Yes, there might be something there.'

'I think that's the one. The fog is a good thing in a way, as if we could see all those islands at once it would be even more confusing. Quick, bear away.'

A large wave was rearing up on the beam, but Tom got our stern into it in time.

'Sorry, didn't see that one. They're all coming from different directions.'

'Bouncing off the cliffs. I'd better assemble the oars in case anything goes wrong. The entrance looks pretty narrow. There will be one hell of a sea in it.'

This was a desperate landfall. We were committed to a narrow cut between high cliffs, from which there could be no escape. If it was the right one, we would be saved. If it was the wrong one, we would be smashed onto the rocks. I started going rigid with fear, and hoped Tom would not notice. I stared hard at the gap. There were vertical

Tom pumping out.

Tom writing up the deck log while at the helm.

granite cliffs either side. In the middle was a boiling sea of white water, shooting up the cliffs. What was on the other side? There was not a cliff, so it looked like we would come out the other side. But how could I be sure there were no submerged rocks? There was no way of telling, except that the chart showed none. If we were wrong, we would not be able to beat back out. It was getting late in the evening, and there was no way we could thread these narrow gaps in the dark. This was our last chance to find shelter for the night.

We entered into the gap, with granite cliffs and few yards either side of us, and spray shooting up them as the big Atlantic waves broke. Five minutes later we were safely through the gap and found ourselves in calm water surrounded by about six islands. We tied up on the lee side of an island called Tan.

We walked over to the windward side to admire the sea and collect driftwood. Then I got a fire going while Tom cooked a beef curry.

Tom had proved to be a really first-rate crew. For most of the cruise we had been splitting responsibilities equally, and I had complete confidence in his ability to handle the boat and navigate when I was asleep off watch. Tom said he had been sailing since before he was born, so this explained his sailing skills. He was also another of those remarkable people, like Barry, who never lost his temper.

Much as we liked these remote islands offshore, we decided to sail to a town to restock with provisions. So we sailed to a delightful town on the mainland called Hunnebostrand. Another fast wet passage and we were reefed again. Visibility was better, but the seas were worse. High and confused – like a tide race, but in fact it was a clapotis effect of waves rebounding off cliffs. There was one wave which swept over the bows in a vertical wall about three feet above the foredeck. I got my fair share of it under the spray cover. Tom was steering in the worst of it and described it in the log:

Calypso planing on very confused sea – one or two nasty breakers that needed handling with respect. Both very anxious – PRC because of tricky navigation and TWM trying to steer appropriate course – v. difficult in these seas.

There were a lot of unmarked rocks and shallows some way offshore, but position fixing was not accurate as we could only take hand bearings from the top of a wave, about eight feet up. Most of the time, the waves rose high above us and blocked our view. Again, accurate course keeping was essential.

Eventually we dropped the reefed main and ran in through the islands under genoa alone. Hunnebostrand was set in magnificent surroundings: steep high rocks on a barren coastline and the houses all made of wood, with big eaves and bright colours. The houses were mostly painted red, and many of them were on stilts, with the water lapping underneath them. This felt like an undiscovered jewel. We arrived just before the shops closed, so I rushed off to get more provisions and Camping Gaz. I returned to find Tom busy answering questions from an attentive crowd that had formed around *Calypso*. This sort of thing became a regular feature of visiting ports. Our every move was watched for hours. A lot of people knew who we were from the press coverage.

We discovered that one of the stringers under the floorboards had cracked, allowing the plywood bottom to come loose. This must have happened while *Calypso* was pounding and planing through the confused seas earlier on. So we spent most of the next day repairing this and a number of other things that had had too much rough treatment.

Swept away in the night

We left in the evening, and for the next four days sailed northwards 'inside', along the narrow channels between the Swedish islands, sailing during the daytime and anchoring off uninhabited islands at night. Most of the time, the weather was as depressing as you can

On a Swedish anchorage.

get – poor visibility, and incessant rain varying from the gentlest drizzle to a deluge under a thunderstorm. But there were two consolations – the scenery was very beautiful, and navigation was much easier than expected as the channels were up to 700 feet deep and most of the dangerous submerged rocks were marked.

We had been surprised by the lack of yachts at sea, and now we knew why – they all cruised in these inshore channels, and from the number of them it seemed that every Swede must own either a small yacht or a varnished, clinker-built, traditional motorboat. It was a wonderful cruising ground, with countless anchorages, numerous deserted islands, easy navigation, and negligible tides. What more could we want?

The boat was nearly wrecked one night. We were anchored close to a rocky island, with our bows tied onto the rock. The wind had freshened, and the anchor holding our stern off the rocks dragged. The bows were still tied to the rocky island and I was woken by the boat banging against the rocks. I woke Tom, who stowed our sleeping bags and cooking gear, while I pulled in the anchor and tried to fend off. I went ashore to cast off the bow line, then shoved off and leapt onto the boat as Tom started rowing, sitting inside the tent. I made a major mistake in not taking the tent down before casting off, but we had to get away from the rocks quickly, and there was not enough time. Also, the tent would keep the sleeping bags dry from the pelting rain. We would have to row like Roman galley slaves, unable to see the blades of our oars.

Tom was unable to see the oar blades in the darkness outside the tent, and an oar was lost overboard. It was a dark night, blowing half a gale and raining, and we were drifting towards a lee shore – rocks and cliffs about a mile away. What could we do now? We could not control our course or direction. One oar was as good as none. We would be wrecked within half an hour.

'I'll try to cast the anchor,' I suggested.

'It's too deep,' Tom replied. 'The warp's 120 feet and the water is deeper than that.'

'It's our only option,' I said. 'It might get shallower as we close the rocks.'

Calypso was making fast progress backwards under the windage of the mast and the tent. I leaned over the bow to cast the anchor on its full length of 120 feet of warp. It never gripped. It was just getting dragged under the boat. I tried three more times, each time hauling in all 120 feet of warp before casting again, and each time it failed to grip. We could see the rocks in the darkness, with the surf breaking on them. It would be the end of the boat, and of our voyage.

'I'll jump over and swim for it,' Tom shouted. 'You should do the same. You might survive even if the boat is destroyed.' I could now hear the roar of the breakers. We would be smashed in a few seconds.

My fifth cast would have to be the last, as we were almost on the rocks.

I felt a tug on the anchor warp. 'It's touching the bottom, Tom!' Then it tugged hard and the boat spun round. It gripped when we were about 20 yards from the rocks. We were saved. If it had not gripped, we would have been destroyed in the black night. We kept an anchor watch in case the anchor dragged, until the wind died down at dawn. We found the oar washed up on the shore near us.

Light all night

Finally we crossed the border and set out across the open sea for the last time before sailing into the Oslofjord. The skies cleared when we got into Norwegian waters, and we sailed on through the night in the lightest of light breezes, looking for wind with wet fingers and pipe smoke. We had a glorious sunset which stayed in the north all night and gradually turned into a sunrise. It was a very cold morning, and I woke up shivering inside all the clothing I had, including an Arctic suit and the big waterproof sleeping bag. We arrived at Larkollen at 0615, and later looked up Bjørn and Marie Christine Egers, whom I had met in Kiel. We spent a hot sunny day in Larkollen, taking their daughter Nina and another girl out for a sail, sunbathing, swimming and collecting oysters. *Calypso*'s interior dried out inside for the first time for a week, and it made living on board her quite pleasant again. This was our first taste of Norway: beautiful fjords, hospitable people, in spite of their Viking ancestors, and another language to learn, slightly different from Swedish.

It took us three more days to sail and row up the Oslofjord, and we had a repeat of the weather conditions of the previous few days – grey skies and drizzle. During this time we perfected the teamwork necessary for the various chores. At the start of the voyage it used to take about two hours to get going in the morning, as so much had to be stowed and unstowed, rather like a game of solitaire. But by now we had cut this to fifteen minutes. We had also speeded up the process of converting *Calypso* from a sailing dinghy to a cabin, with cooker, radio, gas light, air beds and so on all in use. The tent could now be unstowed and up in two and a half minutes.

The first day we saw a yacht becalmed near us, so rowed over to offer them a tow. The owner was a chap called Tore Ringvold, the yacht a racing International One Design, and he had had his outboard motor stolen. He came on board *Calypso* and helped row while I steered his yacht behind. After an hour, some wind sprang up and we parted, but we met up with him again in Oslo.

The next day saw us rowing and sailing further up the Oslofjord in grey skies and drizzle. We raced a German yacht up the fjord. He hoisted his spinnaker first, but when we hoisted ours he got to windward of us and blanketed us very well with a sail area about four times the size of ours. We told him we would overtake him in five minutes, so bore away, then hardened up under his stern and ended up in a luffing match.

After five minutes, he shouted, 'Tell me, are all English sailing boats as slow as yours?'

After another ten minutes we asked, 'Are all German yachts as slow as yours?' Then we put the genoa up as well to catch the wind between foredeck and spinnaker – and as we drew away we waved a rope and asked if he'd like a tow.

We eventually reached Oslo on the afternoon of 29 July. We celebrated in the evening by sitting down to our first proper meal since leaving Kiel. We had had enough of dehydrated curry.

Tom left on 31 July, hitchhiking into the Arctic to see the midnight sun, then south to catch the ferry from Esbjerg. I had to find some work in Oslo to pay for freight to get the boat back to England. I got in touch with Tore Ringvold, and his way of finding me a job was to contact Norway's biggest national newspaper, *Aftenposten*, to write an article about the trip and mention that I was looking for work in Oslo. The journalist turned out to be an attractive young Norwegian blonde. She titled the piece '*Roret brakk tre ganger*' (the rudder broke three times).

Working as a docker to pay for a trip to the Arctic

I got some work down in the docks. Some was gruesome – washing filthy trucks covered in salt, mud and oil – and most of it was back-breaking dock labouring. This was before the widespread use of containers, and everything was lifted out of the ships' holds in slings. We often carried the smaller loads along the dockside, usually between two of us. I soon learned the Norwegian words for 'put it down', and longed to hear those words. It was a way to appreciate the hard life of a labourer. For me, it was an experience; for them, a lifetime of misery. The best job was driving new cars, still covered in wax, off a car ship, up winding lanes like those in a multi-storey car park. For a teenager without a car, this was fun.

When unemployed, I would sit in *Calypso* in the sun writing up the account of the trip for *Yachting World* magazine. The weather during the next three weeks was phenomenal: virtually cloudless with the temperature in the eighties and nineties. For days Oslo was the hottest capital in Europe! *Calypso* turned into a sort of convertible flat, with the tent rolled back in the daytime. I once held an

In Oslo – suit and tie hung up in *Calypso*.

all-night party on her – five of us, including two Norwegian girls, an Irishman and a Dutchman. They say you can use the Wayfarer for almost anything, and we did!

Then on 11 August I set off hitchhiking over three thousand miles into the Arctic. Early on, I was given a lift, and the driver told me he was 'only going 20 miles'. I could not believe my luck when we were still going after over 100 miles. I later learned that a Norwegian mile is six British miles. It was a wonderful experience, travelling on dirt roads through snow-capped mountains, past fjords where one could fish or swim (for a few minutes), sleeping under the heavens at night.

One night I slept on the rocks at Saltstraumen, where the tides run at up to 22 knots, the strongest in the world. It was a fantastic sight, with the water boiling and eddying through a narrow gap at the mouth of a huge fjord. The story goes that a Second World War German warship was built to be able to go against this current and therefore seek shelter in the Saltfjord in any conditions. When it was tested, the current spun it through 90 degrees so that each end was on the rocks, and broke the ship in two.

Calypso stowed down in *Kari K.*

Finally I made it to Hammerfest, which prides itself on being the world's northernmost city, where it was light all night, then on through desolate Arctic terrain. The fjords in the Arctic were stunning. The further north I went, the better the scenery was.

It was getting very cold at night, and I had no tent or sleeping bag, so I bought a reindeer skin for £2, and slept under it in Lapland. Then south through the pines and lakes of Sweden back to Oslo.

Back home to *Calypso* in Oslo, where Vesta curries, coffee, air beds and so on were the height of luxury after ten days without tent or sleeping bag, living mostly on bread and milk. I spent three more weeks in Oslo, doing more manual work at the docks, earning enough to keep myself and *Calypso* in reasonable condition and get us both home. I had some lovely days sailing on the Oslofjord with a Norwegian girl called Kari Minde, but the summer soon came to an end and it was time to go home. By this time I was sleeping inside two sleeping bags with all of my Arctic clothing on and beginning to dream of what it must be like to have a hot bath and sleep in a real bed again.

Calypso and I returned on a small cargo vessel, the *Kari K.* The boat was wedged in a space amongst bags of cargo, and I had the medical unit berth. There was fog most of the trip. We were back in UK three months after leaving the Kent coast.

Calypso is a two-person cruising Wayfarer, and the other members of the crew contributed more than anything else to the success of the cruise. Barry and Tom were very different, but they had this in common: they were very competent and reliable, and they were tolerant by nature – a very important factor when two people are enclosed in a space eight feet by five for such a long time.

Calypso had proved herself again in a variety of conditions – sliding down the shingle at Deal, planing hour after hour in the North Sea, rowing through locks, lakes and canals, into the heart of Amsterdam, into Copenhagen on a hair-raising night, and up the Swedish islands in rare conditions of fog and heavy weather. She had been a sailing dinghy for 1,200 miles and a home for 80 days.

At the time, it was believed that this 1,200-mile journey was the longest ever undertaken by a class sailing dinghy anywhere in the world. The trip attracted a lot of publicity, both in the newspapers and in the shape of more articles in *Yachting World* magazine. *Yachting World* had a long history, since 1894, and was the most widely distributed sailing magazine in the world, reaching over 100 countries. A British newspaper covered the story under the title 'Off to German job in sixteen-foot dinghy'. Wayfarer sales got a big boost from all this coverage, and many people were introduced to sailing as a result. That in itself made it all worthwhile. It was equally gratifying to discover that people still remembered these trips, and the publicity they generated, over 45 years later.

6

More Atlantic Adventures

Could we cross the Atlantic?

Whilst at Cambridge, I reconnected with Rob Collister, an old friend from my boarding school who was now living close to my digs. Rob was an enthusiastic mountaineer who went on to become a professional guide. His experience of sailing was limited to the Norfolk Broads but at least he knew about being cold and wet for long periods. He often went to the Himalayas to climb first ascents. I'd been on a training expedition with him in Scotland at the end of a winter, and seen him in action. He was due to go to Antarctica for two years as an expedition guide for scientists. While talking to him in May 1969, before my trip to Scandinavia, I mentioned that I thought it feasible to sail *Calypso* across the Atlantic via the Trade Winds. This would be the first ocean crossing by a class dinghy. Much to my surprise, he was interested in doing this. We decided to do some trials before he left for Antarctica. I even started thinking of sailing *Calypso* in the Arctic or Antarctic, and how to haul her out onto the pack ice with an anchor and tackle, but this was clearly pipe dreaming.

There was a lot to be done. I wanted to meet someone who had sailed in the Trades, to find out how strong they were, and what sorts of seas I could expect. I approached Sir Francis Chichester, then a legend after his record-breaking solo voyage around the world. As a result of this, I got a letter in January 1970 from him. He wrote, 'I should like to meet you. Could you telephone this office on Monday morning and make a date with me?' I met him at his map business

Rob Collister.

office at St James Place in London. He was a wiry, weathered man, with a slow, calculating voice, and he exuded immense confidence. I was admiring a photo of a colossal wave in the Southern Ocean, and he said, 'That was a nice sunny day.' He told me that the Trades were generally force 4, but could reach force 6–7 in squalls. 'This would not be good for you if this happened at night,' he said.

The Royal Southern Yacht Club asked me to give a slideshow and lecture on 24 January 1970, which would help with publicity and sponsorship. Then, a breakthrough. Ian Proctor wrote saying that he was happy to modify the Wayfarer design, allowing the rudder to be vertical. This would reduce loads, and help prevent more breakages. I became the Wayfarer Class Owners' Association cruising secretary on the executive committee, and was able to see this modification through.

I wrote to a number of organisations for sponsorship, not for the Atlantic, which would happen about 1973, and was still top secret, but for another offshore cruise, ideally west Scotland to the remote islands of St Kilda in 1970. As we often sipped brandy to keep warm on night watches, I wrote to Hine Cognac. I got a reply, saying, 'Unfortunately I cannot see how our principals could benefit from your exploits. In addition, the image we are aiming to preserve for Hine Cognac is one of extreme quality, and I feel that high quality and connoisseurship is less appropriate for your sort of activity than strength and the ability to keep out the cold.' However, they did send me a bottle of cognac.

Our trial sail was to be in the Channel, as Rob did not have time for the Atlantic off Scotland. We attempted two crossings to France, but were driven back each time by bad weather. On our second attempt, I was alarmed to see strong, straight jetstream cirrus, then a halo, a sure sign of something evil coming up. The 1355 shipping forecast was for a force 8 gale where we were, caused by a vicious secondary low swooping down from Iceland. It would hit us during the night. We had no option but to run back to England. We hove to to fix our position with the RDF. I listened to the whine of the radio earplugs, swivelling the unit to and fro looking for the null, as the wind noise picked up. Casquets was 50 degrees, St Catherine's Point 60 degrees. I could just make out the white cliffs of Old Harry Rocks at 345 degrees, and that fixed our position. We set a course of 20 degrees to the Needles and surfed our way back with eight rolls in the main. When we got to the Needles Channel, we had a 4-knot fair tide under us, whipping us through vicious overfalls in Hurst Narrows. As soon as we reached the smoother waters of the Solent, the inevitable curry was cooked.

Shortly afterwards, Rob sailed for Antarctica. He wrote to me, saying he'd just read Nansen's *Greenland* (the account of the first crossing in 1888). I was amazed when Rob wrote that he thought I was 'in the same mould' as Nansen, as I had idolised Nansen since I was a boy.

After graduating, I lived in the deserts of Abu Dhabi for four years. I worked in the Arabian Empty Quarter, driving Land Rovers through dunes up to 1,000 feet high. Temperatures reached record levels, up to 59 degrees Celsius in the shade. We sometimes wore gloves for lunch inside tents, as the knives and forks were too hot to touch. One of my projects involved a temperature survey, and I measured over 80 degrees Celsius in the sun.

The dune seas were like a stormy ocean: towering, red-coloured, majestic and moving relentlessly south-east. Each big one had hundreds of smaller ones on its back, and a huge slip-face on its front, which let out a deep thundering noise if you drove down it. I got to know and admire the Bedu, who were the only people who understood the sands. Expats never managed to match their driving and navigational skills. Navigation was entirely by dead reckoning, distinguishing one dune from another, and above all being able to retrace your journey backwards – often difficult if tracks had been blown out, or dune shapes required a tortuous route. At night, this was very hard, as everything was black outside the narrow beam of the headlights, and the risk was always getting into an area from which it was impossible to get out – the worst being deep blow-holes downwind of slip faces. I got lost and had to head back across uncharted dunes. I was overturned once, and stranded all night.

I sometimes sailed to a deserted island, where the shallow water was too hot to put a foot in without being scalded. I also took up scuba diving, which was in deeper, cooler water, and did some professional salvage work, as I had the only air compressor in the country.

I made further plans for the Atlantic. Water would be a big problem, and we planned to stow it in plastic bottles under the floor-boards. Could we get across before it ran out? Would the weight of it (115kg, not much less than the weight of the boat) prevent the boat from sailing properly? I thought of installing extra buoyancy around the outside of the boat. There were hundreds of other items on my lists, mainly modifications to the boat to allow it to do something it was never intended to do. A comprehensive testing programme was planned, including capsizing with everything on board, even at night (when it is most likely to happen).

During this time, Rob had a dangerous crisis in Antarctica, when his sledge and dogs broke through the sea ice. After seven hours scrambling on ice floes, he got frostbite on his knees, fingers and toes. When he got back to the UK, both his family and my family pressured us to call it off. In retrospect, it was a wise decision, as a capsize would have been very likely, and probably fatal.

Swept away after the oar broke

I finished my work in Abu Dhabi, and in the autumn of 1974 I moved to Aberdeen to work offshore in the North Sea and the North Atlantic, north and west of the Shetlands. I was amazed at the size of the winter seas, which could exceed 90 feet high and a quarter of a mile long. They would smash the undersides of the drilling rigs

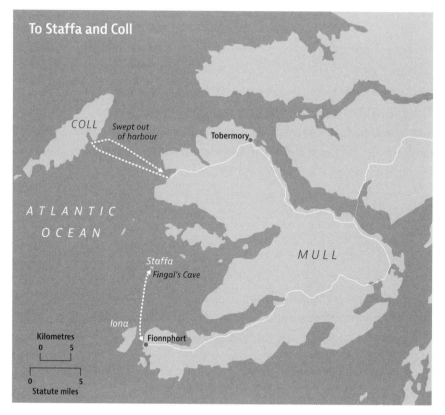

To Staffa and Coll.

and platforms that I worked on. Many people were killed every year, often when entire rigs weighing thousands of tonnes were capsized. Once we landed in a helicopter in a force 12, 60-knot hurricane-force winter storm, on the helideck of a rig that was heaving over 30 feet up and down. The pilot slammed it down at the top of a wave, and held reverse thrust hard while we had a short meeting, then we were off again before the fuel ran out.

I did get some sailing in on *Calypso* during the summers. The summer in northern Scotland lasts only a couple of months. July and August are officially summer, but are usually torn up by wet, windy depressions. I stored the boat on a farm. The mast was snapped off by a tractor, requiring me to install another one, our third.

The beginning of the 1977 summer was beautiful. I trailed *Calypso* behind an Austin Healey 3000 sports car, top down, shirt off, on a hot still day – stares from villagers, pink rhododendrons, pale green glacial valleys. I was travelling with an American friend, Joyce Bergen. We crossed the Sound of Mull on the Lochaline ferry, then drove along twisting narrow roads to Fionnphort.

We launched and sailed to the Isle of Staffa. A black shadow indicated the entrance to a cave. We downed sails and rowed in – the blue swell lapping the walls at the entrance, all the way to the back. The mast just fitted in. Then there was an eerie sound, wailing and groaning: a cormorant croaking, distorted by the weird acoustics in the cave.

The next few days were spent on a leisurely drive around the west and north of Mull, and day sailing under a cloudless sky. A fine reach to the island of Coll ended up with nine rolls in the main and no jib as the wind freshened. I decided to move *Calypso* to a better mooring. It was hard work rowing into such a wind – no progress at all, then the port oar broke and we were swept out of the bay doing 4 knots under bare poles, trying to ship the rudder before being wrecked.

What could we do now? I could not sail or row back to Coll. There was no option but to run for it back to Mull on a fast planing reach with the Cuillin mountains silvery and distant on our port beam. I had checked into a bed and breakfast on Coll, but was never to return, which must have raised questions about what happened to us.

The next venture was from Findhorn on the north coast of Aberdeenshire. Findhorn has a sailing club, so I went in to find out about how to get over the bar at the entrance. 'Bar? Oh yes, the bar! I believe it's moved in the last couple of years.' Nobody else in the clubhouse knew much about it, although they seemed very familiar with the one they were sitting round. At least it hadn't moved.

As it turned out, there was only 12–18 inches of water over the bar and no one was out sailing. Once outside we reefed and set a course for the other side of the Moray Firth. A blue crisp day turned into a thick grey one. We arrived in time for an evening beer at the local. At the end of the return passage it was dark and gloomy. However, we hit the coast at the right place towards midnight and had a desperate beat against the ebbing Findhorn estuary.

On the drive back to Aberdeen at night, *Calypso* came loose and overtook the car. She ploughed through a hedge and was extricated with the help of some RAF pilots on the way back from a booze-up. A blown tyre and a long search for petrol meant that we didn't get back to Aberdeen till daybreak.

The summer was rounded off with some day sailing out of Stonehaven – one day with some Australian friends, Richard and Kay, with their two-year-old daughter Carly. I tried to dissuade Kay from coming, since it was blowing a force 6 from the south.

'Don't worry, Peter, we'll be all right.' Kay had been a cook in the Sydney–Hobart race. With nine rolls in the main, and with Kay and Carly tied together, we sailed out to sea. Sanity, seasickness and several soakings caused Kay to volunteer a return to shore. Carly summed it up with her comment, 'The Clutterboat is wet.'

Richard and I then went out again, 5–10 miles out and down the coast. We had some fast surfing on the way back, with the wind building to force 7, looking at the grey-black seas breaking against the sandstone cliffs below Dunnottar Castle.

The summer was over.

Calypso crosses the Atlantic

After four years working the North Sea, I transferred with BP to work in Alaska, living just north of San Francisco. I raced catamarans on the Pacific coast, and then bought an offshore racing yacht, completing the singlehanded Great Pacific Longitude Race (LongPac) and the Singlehanded Transpacific Race (TransPac). I was lucky to be making good money from the Alaska work, and my racing keelboat was able to handle ocean conditions in its stride. Compared to *Calypso*, this was easy, with a cabin to keep the seas outside, satellite and Loran navigation, and no chance of a capsize given the big lead keel underneath. The challenge for the singlehanded races was handling a big yacht designed for a crew of eight. Sleeping off watch with no-one on the helm took some getting used to. The big spinnakers were really hard work, and a nightmare if the self-steering systems did not work.

I became a good friend of Peter Bird, who was the first person to row across the Pacific. Sadly he died in a storm while rowing back

Video glimpses of *Calypso* in San Francisco Bay.

from Japan to California. He was an inspirational adventurer, with a wicked sense of humour.

Calypso did eventually cross the Atlantic. She was shipped out in a 20-foot container, which required sawing the top off the 22-foot mast and welding it back on. I rebuilt the boat a second time, as she was now 20 years old. I had some great day sailing on San Francisco Bay. *Calypso* was used for a learn-to-sail video that I produced, called *The Sixty Minute Sailor*, which ended up in many libraries and collections over the next quarter-century. I was delighted that the boat had helped teach so many people to sail. I was amused to learn that it had ended up in the adult section of a video store, as the management thought it was about 60 minutes of a sailor's activities in a red light district. Apparently, it was in hot demand, and was in a plain cover which gave no idea of its contents. They had no intention of moving it to the sports section, as it was selling well in the adult section. I hope that it changed many lives, by teaching people about sailing when they were expecting something rather different.

I sailed back from San Francisco to the UK, down the Pacific coast, stopping at the fabled Cocos Island with its high waterfalls and hammerhead sharks, through Panama, then across the Atlantic. I was by now a professional yachtsman, running a charter, delivery and sailing school business, and I had the good fortune to do this 14,000-mile journey as skipper of a 65-foot ketch. I was also sailing back to my career base in the oil industry: next, postings in the UK, Middle East and South America; later, Russia and Africa. On the long night watches, I reflected on what *Calypso* had brought me, both in sailing experience, and in developing my skills for a career in the energy industry. There were common features in adventure, travel, navigation, crises, challenges and rewards. In fact, one of the reasons that I had got selected for my first oil industry job was that the interview team felt that the dinghy voyages proved that I could work in a hostile environment. What had started as a teenage adventure led to many opportunities.

Epilogue

When I moved back to England in 1989, *Calypso* came too, and was based at the Hayling Island Sailing Club on Chichester Harbour, where she had come from nearly 30 years before. I sailed with my parents (the first time in *Calypso* for my mother), with my wife Bonnie, and with my two sons, Mike and Rich, who learned to sail on her. Bonnie had sailed with me across the Pacific and Atlantic, and found *Calypso* a bit nerve-wracking by comparison. I also did two more cruises, with my brother Julian.

The first cruise was to the Isles of Scilly. We had a job finding these flat islets, which were below the horizon in poor visibility,

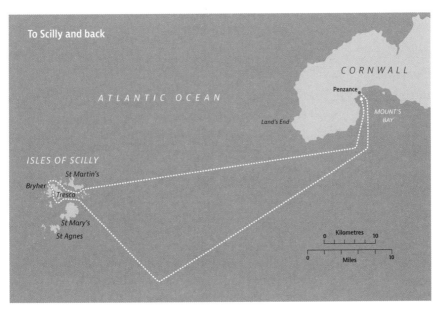

To Scilly and back.

Bonnie and Mike in Ireland.

and nearly missed them. The cruising in the clear, shallow waters between the islands was just superb. One day, we went outside, back into the Atlantic, and faced steep, big seas breaking against cliffs.

The other cruise was off the south-west coast of Ireland, including a rounding of the Fastnet Rock, using GPS this time. Sailing here was breathtaking, navigating wild, rocky shores and negotiating narrow channels. There were some tide rips sweeping out into the open waters, adding to the drama. Even the names were awe-inspiring, such as Roaringwater Bay.

The boat was rebuilt twice more, the second time by Ian Porter. After nearly 50 years, she was better than new, and had a vastly improved sail handling system, with roller jib and slab-reefed mainsail, which was much faster, and allowed a better set when reefed. The mainsheet could now be centre-sheeted, which was much more controllable. I also put in a trapeze, allowing me to sail singlehanded.

In the 1990s, most of my sailing was on a 43-foot Grand Prix offshore trimaran called *Spirit of England*, mainly double-handed ocean racing in the Atlantic. I sailed mostly with Brian Thompson,

In the Isles of Scilly.

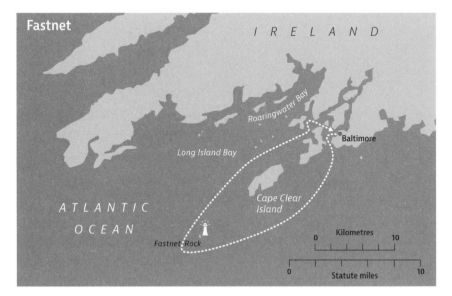

Fastnet.

one of the world's top ocean racing sailors. We won fifteen races and broke four international records.

Spirit sailed waters described in this book over a dozen times, often at speeds over 20 knots. It was a totally different experience from that in *Calypso*: in a leading offshore multihull, able to take rough conditions in its stride, with reliable weather forecasts, accurate navigation, and long-distance communications equipment. It was like going down a bumpy dirt road in a Grand Prix Formula 1 race car, compared with previous trips on a mountain bike. The main common factor was risk of capsize.

While racing with John Chaundy, the trimaran was dismasted and holed in five places, at night in the mid-Atlantic. We survived by building a jury rig while lying to an eighteen-foot-wide parachute anchor. It took us ten days to build a jury rig and reach land.

I also worked for a decade in East Africa, enjoying some fine sailing and scuba diving in the Indian Ocean. I started mountaineering, which took me to the Alps, the Himalayas, Alaska, Greenland, Africa and the Andes. I flew over Cape Horn in a Russian cargo plane on an expedition to an unexplored mountain region in Antarctica. I did some sailing there – kite skiing.

Mike and Rich.

Calypso became a family boat, and took out three generations of us in coastal waters – exactly what the Wayfarer had been designed to do. My sons came out sailing with me, often from Hayling Island to the Isle of Wight. It was fantastic to be able to share with them the joys of sailing an open dinghy across a sparkling sea. Barry and I went for a 44-year reunion sail in Chichester Harbour in 2012. Both of us agreed that we were lucky not to have had a fatal disaster on those earlier adventures.

Back in Chichester Harbour.

Part 2

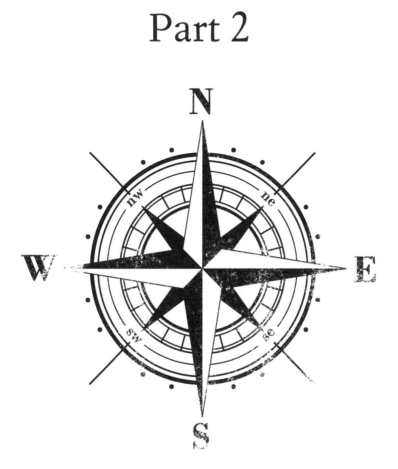

Some of the information in this section is specific to the Wayfarer dinghy. Many of the principles may also be applied to other boats.

Modifications to a Dinghy
for Sailing Offshore

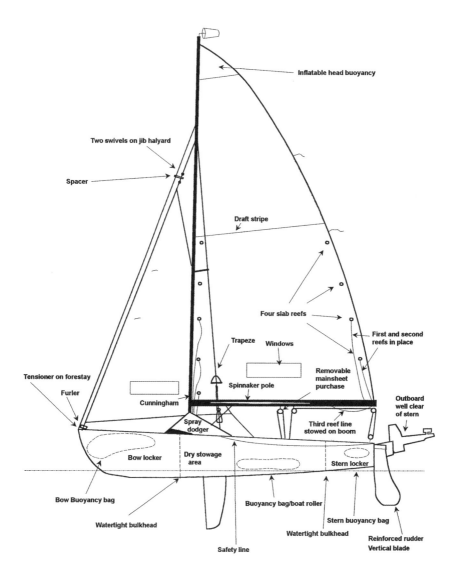

Inflatable head buoyancy

Two swivels on jib halyard

Spacer

Draft stripe

Four slab reefs

First and second
reefs in place

Trapeze   Windows

Removable
mainsheet
purchase

Tensioner on forestay

Furler

Cunningham

Spray
dodger

Spinnaker pole

Outboard
well clear
of stern

Third reef line
stowed on boom

Bow locker

Dry stowage
area

Stern locker

Bow Buoyancy bag

Buoyancy bag/boat roller

Stern buoyancy bag

Watertight bulkhead

Watertight bulkhead

Reinforced rudder
Vertical blade

Safety line

Sailing gear

These modifications can be removed to allow racing within class regulations.

Oversized and backup fittings (shroud, chainplate, rudder etc)
This is because the shock loads caused by waves are much higher than design loads.

Four slab reefs
This system is much easier to operate than the boom furler system we originally had, and also results in a flatter mainsail set, which is essential when reefed. Our system is all on auto-jamming cleats, so that it can be operated with one hand. The same goes for cunningham, kicking strap and outhaul. It is essential that the helmsman can operate all this singlehanded, and at night, so as to be able to shorten sail rapidly without waiting for a half-conscious off-watch crew to attempt to help from a deep sleep. The reefing system must also allow for a complete drop of the mainsail in heavy weather, with lines for

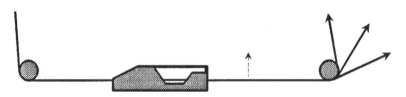

Auto-jamming line cleat.

Slab reefs to leech.   Slab reefs and furler.

lashing the mainsail to the boom. A centre-mainsheet system is also compatible with slab reefs.

Variable-purchase mainsheet

Our mainsheet has two pulley blocks with rotating cheeks, which allow the purchase to be varied from low (for light winds or off wind) to high (for heavy weather or upwind). The key is to be able to dump the mainsheet immediately and spill all the wind. Any delay to this risks a capsize.

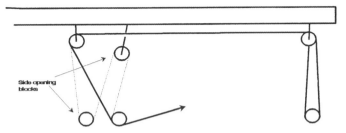

Purchase changing on mainsheet, with side-opening blocks.

Mainsheet set for beating.   Mainsheet set for running.

Mainsheet set for broad reaching.

Jib/genoa furler

This is generally either fully set or fully furled, as the partially furled headsail is too full to be useful. Again, it is on jam cleats, so can be operated with one hand. Also useful for dousing when setting a spinnaker.

Reinforced rudder, lifting hinged tiller

After our many rudder breakages, we modified the rudder extensively. The problem for Wayfarers is less now that the class regulations allow a more vertical rudder. A major problem is that when surfing down big waves, the boat speed is much higher than when planing in sheltered water, even with full racing sail set, so the rudder blade can be forced up, which can easily break the rudder. A locking pin is a way of preventing this. We also have a safety line to the bottom of the blade so that we can retrieve the blade if it snaps off.

A hinged tiller allows access to the stern locker while sailing.

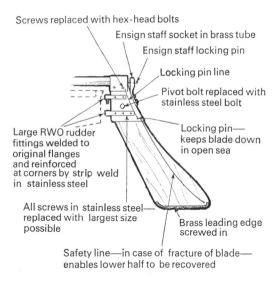

Screws replaced with hex-head bolts

Ensign staff socket in brass tube

Ensign staff locking pin

Locking pin line

Pivot bolt replaced with
stainless steel bolt

Large RWO rudder
fittings welded to
original flanges
and reinforced
at corners by strip weld
in stainless steel

Locking pin—
keeps blade down
in open sea

All screws in stainless steel—
replaced with largest size
possible

Brass leading edge
screwed in

Safety line—in case of fracture of blade—
enables lower half to be recovered

The modified rudder. Class regulations now allow a more vertical rudder than shown here.

Pump (one each side, one via centreboard)

Piston pumps each side allow pumping from the weather side
(usually helmsman), while drawing water from the lee side via
hoses under the floorboards. A bilge pump by the mast is also useful,
pumping into the centreboard case. Powerful self-bailers each side
are also essential.

Pumping out.

Extra stowage, mainly watertight
The principles of stowage are as follows:

+ Everything must be tidy so that ropes cannot tangle, especially important at night.
+ Everything must have a fixed place, so that it can be found readily, again at night.
+ The boat must be able to survive a capsize, so all gear must be in lockers or lashed down with rope or shock cord. Nothing essential should float away, and nothing should move so as to prevent righting.
+ Anything needed under way should be stowed in the cockpit, be readily accessible, and be able to withstand a salt-water barrage of spray, either waterproof or stored in watertight containers. This includes all sailing equipment, navigation gear, cooking gear, change of clothing, emergency gear and so on.
+ Items that might be needed under way can be stored in the stern locker. These items do not need waterproofing. Heavy items should also be stored here instead of in the bow locker, to improve the trim of the boat, reduce pounding, and reduce loads.
+ The bow locker cannot easily be accessed while under way, so it is best for items such as clothing, charts, sleeping bags and so on. We had a shelf below the foredeck for a suit or other shore clothing to be stowed flat and dry. The rest of the gear was lashed down to prevent movement if capsized, thus helping righting.

Spray cover/dodger
A spray cover keeps breaking waves out of the boat, and provides shelter under way for cooking, navigating and so on. Ours has a top which can be rolled out either on the weather side only (for sleeping under way) or on both sides as a quick shelter for sleeping in harbour in fair weather.

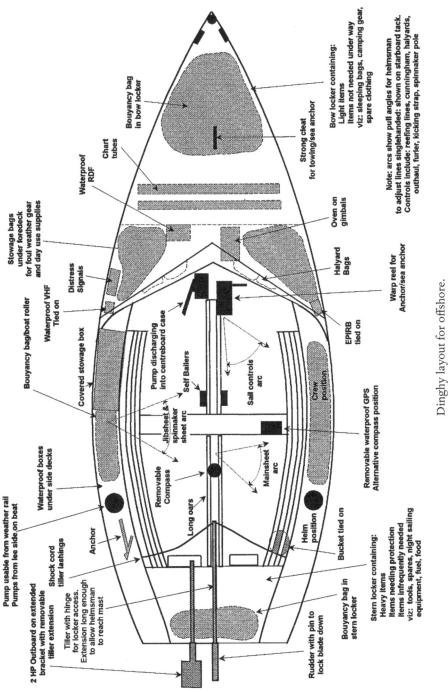

Pump usable from weather rail
Pumps from lee side on beat

2 HP Outboard on extended
bracket with removable
tiller extension

Tiller with hinge
for locker access.
Extension long enough
to allow helmsman
to reach mast

Shock cord
tiller lashings

Waterproof boxes
under side decks

Anchor

Removable
Compass

Long oars

Helm
position

Bucket tied on

Stern locker containing:
Heavy items
Items needing protection
Items infrequently needed
viz: tools, spares, night sailing
equipment, fuel, food

Bouyancy bag in
stern locker

Rudder with pin to
lock blade down

Bouyancy bag/boat roller

Waterproof VHF
Tied on

Distress
Signals

Stowage bags
under foredeck
for foul weather gear
and day use supplies

Waterproof
RDF

Chart
tubes

Bouyancy bag
in bow locker

Strong cleat
for towing/sea anchor

Bow locker containing:
Light items
Items not needed under way
viz: sleeping bags, camping gear,
spare clothing

Covered stowage box

Pump discharging
into centreboard case

Self Bailers

Jibsheet &
spinnaker
sheet arc

Sail controls
arc

Mainsheet
arc

Crew
position

Removable waterproof GPS
Alternative compass position

Oven on
gimbals

Halyard
Bags

Warp reel for
Anchor/sea anchor

EPIRB
tied on

Note: arcs show pull angles for helmsman
to adjust lines singlehanded: shown on starboard tack.
Controls include: reefing lines, cunningham, halyards,
outhaul, furler, kicking strap, spinnaker pole

Dinghy layout for offshore.

171

Spray dodger.

Oars and stern rowlock, outboard

We now have long oars, 8 foot 6 inches. They just fit along the centreline. They cannot be stowed along the side decks, as this is where most of our 'ready access' gear is located. We have also had oars with a joint about halfway along, consisting of a scarf inside a length of steel tubing reinforced with fibreglass. The tubing is attached to the handle half, and the blade half is kept in with a bolt and wing nut passing through the tubing. The blade half can be used as a paddle if there is not time to assemble the oars, and also as an oar for a one-man rubber dinghy. These joints have to take a tremendous strain, particularly when pulling hard in a crisis, so it is important to make a thoroughly strong job of them.

We also have a rowlock fitting on the transom so that an oar can be used as a jury rudder. This has been invaluable on eight rudder breakages. It also allows for the forgotten art of sculling: propelling the boat with an oar off the stern.

Recently, mainly for sailing with children, we have used a 2 HP outboard. This needs to be on a bracket to keep it clear of the rudder. It also needs a tiller extension to allow it to be steered from the cockpit.

Emergency gear
Sea anchor and 120-foot line reel
A sea anchor needs to stop the boat dead, and should be about five feet across, with a parachute design, run off the bows. It needs about 120 feet of stretchy nylon warp, in order to keep the bows into big waves as they surge. The warp should be stowed on a reel by the mast, so that it can be fed out without tangles, day or night. This setup also works well for anchoring in harbour.

Trysail adaptor
This is a strip of canvas the length of the luff of the jib, with a rope sewn along one edge and eyelets along the other. The jib's piston hanks snap into the eyelets, the rope is slotted into the luff groove, and the whole lot hauled up the mast. The 'trysail' is sheeted through the spinnaker-sheet fairleads, which are strong enough for the job. This has worked very well for us when the wind is too strong for a deep-reefed main. It needs a pole from the thwart to raise the clew to get the right shape.

Buoyancy at mainsail head
We have modified the mainsail head so that an inflatable insert can be put in, with enough buoyancy to prevent a 180-degree inversion. It can also be hauled up the mast to provide this function if the mainsail is down.

Side buoyancy bags
These double as fenders, or boat rollers to get the boat up or down a beach. The Wayfarer needs these for stability when full of water after a breaking sea or a capsize.

Navigation
We have a masthead halyard for a navigation light. There is also an extra-high spinnaker-pole eye for a radar reflector.

We use clip-on GPS and compass so that these navigation instruments can be removed when not needed.

Deck logs can be white painted areas suitable for a waterproof Chinagraph pencil, which is all-weather, and used for noting down bearings and DR data such as boat speed and direction.

The radar reflector.

Deck log.

GPS and compass.

Navigating with GPS.

Equipment for living aboard

Tent

Our tent is clipped on with shock cord and snap shackles and can be put up in three or four minutes singlehanded from the cockpit. It uses the shrouds and halyards to get more headroom. It has windows in the bow so that we can see upwind, and see the anchor. I have used it as a home for six weeks at a time after completing a cruise. It is white, to maximise light inside.

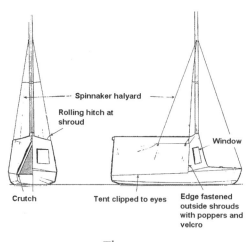

The tent.

Gimballed cooker

We have a small gimballed oven fitted with shelves on which two army mess tins can be mounted one above the other over a single burner, fed from a Camping Gaz (LPG/butane) cylinder in the well forward of the floorboards. It is made of stainless steel, double-walled for insulation and hung under the foredeck. It is ideal for two-pan meals such as curries and other dehydrated food, which is our staple diet while cruising. Should the burner fail, solid fuel can be used instead.

The cooker.

In use.

Offshore Techniques

Safety

Some specific aspects for open boats offshore are as follows.

Fatigue

On a long passage, the crew can get over-tired through lack of sleep. This is extremely dangerous, as it can cause loss of alertness, leading to a capsize by getting off course, having an accidental gybe and so on. It also contributes to navigation errors. The best way around this is to get off watch and rest as much as possible, leaving the boat to be sailed essentially singlehanded. Watch systems can either be rigid (2 on – 2 off, up to 4 on – 4 off), or flexible. I prefer the flexible system, whereby the on-watch crew sails as long as he/she wants, and then calls up the other crew. This can be several hours during the day, down to as little as 15 minutes when very tired at night. The worst thing is to try to complete a rigid watch at night when very fatigued.

Capsize

This is the ultimate nightmare, and likely to be fatal in heavy weather, or at night. The off-watch crew has no chance if asleep on the floorboards, jammed under the thwart. Righting a dinghy at night is unlikely to be successful. In big seas, the boat will swamp faster than it can be bailed out. To reduce the risk of capsize, the boat must be reefed down early, be kept under control downwind so as to avoid a broach, and be capable of instant depowering in any circumstances: at night, while cooking, and during chaotic conditions. All sheets need to be kept tidy, and loose items stowed, to eliminate risk of tangles. Capsize recovery by using the centreboard and sheets over the weather side is the standard approach, but almost impossible at night or in big seas.

Lee shores

These are especially dangerous for a dinghy offshore, as there is no engine, and often the boat cannot get to weather in a strong blow or big seas. Careful planning is needed to avoid any chance of such a situation, by keeping upwind as a tactical measure, so as to be able to bear off rather than be forced to head up. If a lee-shore emergency is unavoidable, then the only option is to select the best location, such as a beach, or a sloping rocky area, and definitely not a cliff. In light conditions, the anchor can save the day if an emergency is caused by broken gear, tides etc.

Man overboard (MOB)

This is much more serious in a dinghy than a keelboat, as it is very difficult for the singlehander left on board to manoeuvre under sail, and at the same time to keep a watch on the crew member in the water. We generally regarded it as certain death. Avoidance is through disciplined use of lifelines, especially at night. Leading the line to the bow would help stop the boat by bringing it head-to-wind, as the MOB would act as a sea anchor. Should MOB happen, the classic response is to gybe onto a reciprocal course, then luff up and pick up from the lee side or transom. The newer technique is to tack onto a hove-to position (i.e. not tacking the jib), and then drift down onto the MOB. This is more practical and safer than a singlehanded gybe. Trailing a line may also help. In big seas, MOB recovery is almost impossible. We rarely wore lifejackets in the 1960s, but we probably should have done. The designs available then did not work well and were often large and clumsy. We relied on lifelines instead, consisting of a rope looped around chest and shoulders.

Shipping

Again, this is much more dangerous in a dinghy, due to small radar image, lack of manoeuvrability, lack of radar on board, and no auxiliary power. Ships generally do not rely on their radar at sea, and are not likely to notice a dinghy. At night, they will not see you, even with a small navigation light. The answer is to keep a very alert lookout, and shine a powerful torch directly at a ship that is coming head on. In fog, a radar reflector is useful, since that is usually the one time when ships rely on their radar. A ship's wash is also dangerous for a dinghy in big seas, especially at night, and you need to be able to predict when it might hit you, as it will confuse big seas.

Heavy weather

As wind builds, it is important to reef early, as it may be too difficult to do when overdue, especially at night. After the first reef, the headsail should be changed to a smaller jib. Second and third reefs can then go in. After that, there is a choice: either drop the main (best if reaching or running), or drop the jib (if beating).

Going upwind in big seas requires luffing each breaking wave, and the boat often stops dead. This is dangerous as there is no steerage control. Also, in the troughs, there may be very little wind to get power into the sails again. Incessant pumping is another problem. In these circumstances, the choices are to run for shelter or lie to a sea anchor.

Going downwind in big seas can be dangerous due to excessive speed, in the 15–20 knot range (twice the planing speed of a dinghy in flat water), and loss of control, with risk of gybe or broach. Both can trigger a capsize. In these conditions, as the wind rises, it may be best to drop the main, then go under bare poles, then lie to a sea anchor.

Above force 6, an open dinghy cannot get to weather. Above force 7, seas build to the point that the boat cannot be sailed at all, and lying to a sea anchor is a solution. In a gale, the boat may still be at risk riding to a sea anchor, and lowering the mast to reduce windage is a solution, as demonstrated by Frank Dye. This requires a block and rope arrangement on the bow to allow this to be done from the cockpit. A cover can be rolled aft on the mast to keep seas out.

Reefing

For both roller and slab reefing, heaving to is the best approach, as it allows singlehanded reefing, and keeps the boat under control. To do this, let the main out, haul the jib to weather, and tie the tiller down to leeward.

Roller reefing is most effective if the boom is tapered to effect a better set and raise the clew. Slab reefing is best done by letting the halyard off to a pre-set mark, then dropping the luff and hauling down, then hauling in the reefing lines on the leach. These should be rigged so that they can be pulled in with one hand, through clam cleats and pulleys. Ideally, reefing should be a singlehanded job. The crew may be asleep. On the Wayfarer, the crew will be on the floorboards, at risk of being trodden on.

Navigation

Navigation technique is much the same as on a yacht, except that one is often working in rain or spray. Relevant pilots, binoculars,

Hove-to.

logbooks, plastic sextant, etc are all stowed in waterproof boxes. A chart table can be made by putting the charts in current use inside a waterproof plastic chart case together with a piece of plywood. We used full-sized Admiralty charts in black and white, much the same as they had been 100 years earlier. The chart can then be put across the knees and plotting done with Chinagraph pencil and protractor. An all-weather deck log is essential so that the helmsman can keep a navigational record.

An illuminated steering compass is essential. A compass bracket with a detachable light can fit onto any part of the thwart. The compass can be detached for hand bearings.

We had a home-made 'Dutchman's log', consisting of 100 feet of line and a float made of a foot length of dowel, painted red and kept upright in the water with a polystyrene float halfway up and a lump of brass at the bottom. The line is attached to the top of the dowel, and yanks it horizontal when the 100 feet is out. A table then converts this time to speed. We also used a Pitot tube held over the side of the boat.

GPS is the ideal tool, as long as it is not relied on (due to risk of battery discharge or damage). Small ones suitable for dinghies can be set up with waypoints in advance.

Before GPS, we used a radio direction finder (RDF), and sometimes astro-navigation. We did the calculations from almanacs, so it was a fair-weather exercise. Pocket calculators can do this, but again it is a fair-weather exercise. We used a sextant more often for vertical angles off landmarks of known elevation, allowing calculation of distance off.

We had no means of communication: no VHF radio, no EPIRB, no mobile phone, and no email. This required us to be very self-reliant, with virtually no chance of a rescue. Today, I would have a portable waterproof VHF, a mobile phone in a waterproof case, and an EPIRB. These would significantly reduce the risks.

Sailing at night

This is a magical experience in a small boat, often under starry skies, with streaks of phosphorescence. The wind is usually steadier than in the day, and less strong. In fair weather, calms are a problem as the wind flows overhead in a laminar fashion.

Keeping everything tidy and stowed is crucial to avoid tangles. After 20 minutes, night vision is well developed, and under a full moon is good enough to read a chart. Plenty of rest and sleep for the off-watch crew is critical, to reduce fatigue. Navigation is often easier due to the longer range of lights offshore, even 30 miles. It is best to plot positions from dead reckoning or bearings, so as to minimise the risk of misinterpreting the situation. In daytime, it is not necessary to do this, as you can get a good 'feel' of where you are. Steering a compass course at night in a dinghy is not easy, and it is better to steer by the feel of the wind, or on a star, if available. It is important to keep well offshore to avoid risks of rocks, reefs, unlit buoys, lobster pots and so on, which can be doom for a dinghy. It is therefore best to approach coastlines after daybreak.

Identification of shipping types and orientation from its lights is crucial, and must be learned by heart, to avoid having to look up a chart or diagram. Today the RYA certification process requires this.

Hypothermia is a problem at night, and high-calorie food is key here, together with one-piece foul-weather gear. This is also useful for sleeping on the floorboards.

Heavy weather should be avoided at night, due to inability to see the waves, or weather changes such as squalls. Fatigue is also much worse, and likely to cause severe accidents.

Living Aboard

Cooking and eating

Cooking is best done when anchored, moored or in harbour. When under the tent, it can be done in any conditions. Hot food stays hot, and there is no risk of an emergency interfering. Our cooker is a double-deck design, suited for cooking on the bottom mess tin, and using the top one to keep previously cooked food warm. It is powered by butane gas, which burns hot, is easy to light, and convenient. However, it is heavier than air, and can sink, causing it to collect in the bilges with an explosion risk. Another problem is corrosion of the burner, gas bottle and fittings.

To cook under way is a big challenge, and cannot be done in any wind or sea upwind, nor in strong breezes downwind. In good conditions, the off-watch crew can cook from the weather side, with the cooker in gimbals. If an 'event' is coming up, such as gybing or reefing, rising wind, shipping etc, then it is best to defer cooking. The simplest cooking is boiling up rice and adding dehydrated food. It can be done inside 20 minutes. Eating is best done one at a time, changing the helm so as not to distract from steering, or heaving to. In heavy conditions, uncooked snack food is the norm, preferably keeping one hand free for the sailing (steering, sheets). We also had emergency self-heating soups, which are cans with a tube inside containing an incendiary device like a firework.

Calorie intake is crucial when offshore in cold weather, especially at night. There are times when a hot meal is critical and justifies dropping sails or heaving to.

The bathroom is fairly basic, consisting of a bucket, best used when hove to if the weather is rough.

Sleeping

Again, there are two cases: in harbour, and while under way. In harbour, a full night's rest is achievable. The Wayfarer has removable side benches, which allows extra sleeping room, head facing aft. We used air mattresses.

Under way, the best you can hope for is a couple of hours at a time – often just a few minutes in heavy conditions. In light conditions, the off-watch crew can get under the thwart and rest on an air bed inside a waterproof sleeping bag, head facing bows. In medium conditions, it is risky to do this due to capsize potential, so the norm is to sleep in one-piece foul-weather gear, with legs over thwart. In heavy conditions, most people would not sleep, and just doze instead on the floor. This allows some rest, and is better than sitting fatigued on the gunwales with the risk of falling overboard.

Stowage List

Some 500 items

In normal sailing positions
Centreboard
Mast and pivot and split pins
Kicking strap and six-part downhaul
Halyards: jib, main, spinnaker, burgee
Forestay and bottlescrew
2 shrouds and 2 safety shrouds
2 bottle screws and 2 safety strops
Rudder, tiller and 3 locking pins
Boom
Genoa and sheets
Mainsail, mainsheet, 4 battens and 2 pulley blocks
Spray cover (2 parts)
Bow hatch
Stern hatch
Burgee, courtesy flags and ensign
Ensign staff
Jib strop

Bow locker
2 bags: spare clothing
Rubber dinghy
2 air beds and 2 sleeping bags
Shelf: shore-going clothing

3 chart rolls (2 plastic and 1 cardboard): up to 35 charts
Waterproof sleeping bag

Cockpit
Compass bracket and steering compass
Navigation light support
Boom crutch
Ropeage hooks: 10ft line, 15ft line, spare jibsheet
Life harness, 2 lifelines
Lifelight: mini sea marker
Tent
Stern steering rowlock
Oven gimbals
2 sets foul-weather gear (plus knife and Chinagraph pencil in each)
1 buoyancy aid, 1 lifejacket
GPS satnav
VHF radio
Large Gaz cylinder
Warp reel and 120ft 1 ton nylon, spindle, nut and wing nut
Large chart case
Small chart case and board
Handbearing compass
2 rowlocks
Signalling torch
Foghorn
Miniflare gun and 7 red flares
Mackerel spinner, weight and 68ft line
2 pneumatic cushions
Anchor, 5ft nylon chain and 5ft steel chain
2 boat rollers
2 paddle sections of oars
2 handle sections of oars and bolt and wing nut
Spinnaker pole

Log float and 150ft line on reel
Reefing claw
2 × 16 gallon per minute pumps and inlet pipes
Flexible pump
Drogue sea anchor
Bucket for trash
2 × 1-gallon water bottles
White flares
Batteries box
Extra flags
Camera in waterproof box: with accessories
Coffee and cutlery box
Chart light in box
Ready-access pilot books: selection for passage
Sextant in waterproof box

Ready-access box
All-weather logbook, Telefix vertical angle instrument, azimuth diagram, chart plotter, pliers, small pieces rope, shock cord, pencils, matches, compass light

Screws box
Copper nails, rivets, piston hanks, eyes, hooks, pulley, bolts, self-tappers, stainless screws, split pins, safety pins, bulldog clips, shackles, spare gooseneck

Clothes net
Drying-up cloth, gloves, miscellaneous clothes (jackets, hats)

Food box (insulated)
Fruit, cheese, chocolate etc

Oven
2 pairs mess tins; hose, fastening and door

Bucket (square)
2 sponge cloths, scourer, scrubbing brush, washing-up brush, detergent, Pitot tube speed indicator

Gaz light
Plus 5 spare mantles, 6 primus prickers, 2 boxes matches and blow torch

Compounds box
Rag, canvas tape, outdoor adhesive, rust paint, elastic waterproof filler, low-melting-point solder, latex solution, Vaseline, whipping twine, cotton, plastic bands, oil, Sellotape, waterproof tape, needles, whippings, plastic bag wires

Torches
2 pocket torches

Binoculars
7 × 50, and case

Navigation box
Reeds Nautical Almanac, ballpoint pens, pencils, Chinagraph pencils, pencil sharpener, logbook, weather chart, RDF headphones, pencil eraser

Emergency rations box
Tube milk, Bovril, 3 bars plain chocolate, concentrated food bar, soup, dextrose/glucose, fudge, waterproof matches

Radio
MW/LW and compass

Tools box
Oiled cloth, round 4-inch file, half-round file, push-drill, twist drills, scraper, small screwdriver and bits, chisel, wire brush, penknife, large G clamp, 2 small G clamps

Signals box
McMurdo sea marker, white flares

Drugs
Milk of magnesia, penicillin, aspirin, caffeine, stomach medicine, seasick pills, codeine, antibiotics

First aid box
Bandage, plasters, scissors, insect repellent, sun cream, burn cream, antiseptic, styptic pencil, tweezers

Stern locker
Small Gaz cylinder
½ gallon rice, ½ gallon macaroni, ½ gallon water
Radar reflector

Sailbag
Spinnaker and 2 sheets, trysail adaptor, small jib

Wooden food box
Assorted drinks – brandy, rum, orange, tin milk, cocoa, 3 self-heating drinks; sugar cubes, 3 plastic boxes eggs, matches, saltwater soap, plastic plates, mustard, chutney, lard, butter, salt, Oxo cubes, lime marmalade, tuna tins, herring, kipper fillet tins

Paints box
Zinc paint, red enamel paint, graphite bottom paint, varnish, 3 brushes, turpentine, filler, wet and dry sandpaper

Fibreglass box
Solvent, 2 tubes filler and catalyst, powder, liquid, plastic gloves, rolls and sheets of glass-fibre matting, catalyst, tar remover, spreader, coarse glass paper, spare forestay and rope end, spare shroud, shock cord

Bag
Solid-fuel cooker for emergencies, dinghy pump and hose, navigation light batteries, foghorn refills, toilet roll, sailmaker's palm, cover centre piece

Ready-access clothes bag
Tracksuit, towel, washing kit etc for use under way

Dried food (in chart cases)
Curries (beef, prawn, chicken, veg), beef risotto, chop suey, chow mein, chicken supreme paella, instant mash, noodles, peas and beans, soy/sweet and sour sauce, raisins, biscuits

Documents
Passport, mobile phone, travellers' cheques, firearms certificate, permanent colour pen, shipping/insurance/bank account papers

Provisions box
Matches, lighter, butane gas cylinder, spare flints, spare batteries, ensign, 6 plastic bags, coffee and cutlery, sugar lumps in box, instant milk, 2 insulated cups, 2 knives, 2 forks, 2 spoons, 1 teaspoon, serrated knife, tin opener/bottle opener, can opener, matches, flags

Glues box
Waterproof glue, impact glue, epoxy glue, Loctite, rubber solution

Spares box
Sailcloth, bailer seal, cooker burner and valve, stainless steel rod, spare hatch clips, scraper blades, torch bulbs, lilo bungs, Velcro, cover cloth, tent cloth, plastic shackle, land compass, bottle screws, zip, sextant mirrors and Allen key, safety walk strip, piston hanks, white light and battery, reflector shield

Personal box
Alarm clock, coins, film

Books and pilots box
Pilots and supplements, graph paper, weather books, paperbacks, Chinagraph pencils, phrase books, dictionaries

Various provisions bag
Patching material for air bed, dinghy, boat roller and oilskins; spare pump hatch cover, spare rubber for hatches, spare rudder fittings, spare mast fittings, waterproof matches

Under floorboards
2 copper tingles, 6 × ½ gallon water bottles

Provisions used in six weeks
2 large + 2 small Gaz bottles
3 × ½ gallon bottles rice, 1 × ½ gallon bottle macaroni
60 two-man curries
20 loaves bread, 20 pkts rye biscuits
15 pkts cheese, 2 tubes jam, 2 jars marmalade
20 gallons water
3 bottles Bacardi, 1 bottle whisky, 2 bottles ginger wine
2 logbooks (about 300 pages in all)

80 eggs
5 pkts butter, 2 pkts lard
3 pkts biscuits, 20 oatmeal biscuits
4 tins herring fillets, sardines, 2 tins tuna
20 cans beer, 6 cans Coca-Cola, 2 bottles orange juice
4 hand torch batteries, 6 signalling torch batteries, 1 radio battery
14 navigation light batteries
3 pkts three-man instant mash, 6 pkts four-man dehydrated vegetables
4 small jars coffee, 6 pkts lump sugar
40 apples, 2 bags walnuts, 3 bags currants
15 bars chocolate
200g salt, 1 bottle chutney
2 bottles detergent
1 can shaving cream, 1 tube toothpaste, 1 bar soap each
4 toilet rolls
4 Chinagraph pencils
1 carbon dioxide cylinder for horn
4 Gaz mantles
140 vitamin pills
2 novels
Plus small amounts: drugs, paints, glues, plasters, matches, fibre-glass etc.

Items which usually wore out or got broken or lost in six weeks

6 ballpoint pens, 4 Chinagraph pencils, 2 cups, 2 chart cases, 10ft shock cord, Scotchbrite cloth, mackerel hook, steering compass, washing-up brush, deck brush, boat roller, oven burner, weather chart, plotting protractor, Gaz Light glass, rudder!

Sailing with Children

I include this section as all my current Wayfarer sailing is with my two sons, Mike and Rich. Extreme offshore sailing in an open boat would not be suitable for anyone under the age of fifteen. However, day sailing and cruising in sheltered waters can be a wonderful – and safe – adventure for children over the age of five.

The main thing to remember is that the motivation of children is entirely different from that of adults. They are not interested in surviving amazing things, conquering the elements, or achieving

objectives. For them, having fun is the key, and learning something. They especially like group settings, with many boats, and other children in their age group. Short passages are the norm, about an hour. Most children enjoy being in charge, and especially steering.

You need to start off in ideal conditions, and work up slowly to rougher settings, or the child can be put off for life. Children get bored, cold and hungry faster than adults, hence the importance of starting with short trips in good weather.

Small children need specially sized lifejackets, and if conditions are rough, children under three can be tied to an adult via a safety harness, rather than to the boat. They should be confident swimmers.

Glossary

Aback. Situation when boat's direction has altered so that the wind is blowing the sails from the opposite side, usually unintended.

Abeam. At right angles to the direction of the boat.

Aft. The rear (stern) end of a boat, or a direction towards that end.

Ahead. In a forward direction.

Almanac. Book containing information about sea areas, ports, aids to navigation, tides and celestial navigation, usually updated annually.

Anchorage. An area suitable for anchoring, sheltered and with good bottom holding ground.

Anticyclone. High-pressure area, with clear weather at its centre, and with clockwise winds in the northern hemisphere.

Astern. In a rear-facing direction.

Astro-navigation. The science of navigating by celestial bodies, usually the sun. Also called celestial navigation.

Azimuth. Direction or bearing; also the direction of a celestial body along the surface of the earth.

Backing. Wind direction changing against the direction of the sun (usually from north-west to south in the northern hemisphere), usually a sign of worsening weather. Opposite to veering, which refers to the wind changing direction with the sun (usually south to north-west in the northern hemisphere).

Bar. Shallow area of sand, typically at the entrance of a river, and often rendering navigation extremely dangerous due to breaking seas.

Batten. Strip of stiff material (often wood) set into a sail at right angles to the leech to improve its shape. There are four on a Wayfarer's mainsail.

Bear away. Turn away from the wind. Opposite to luff up.

Bearing. The horizontal direction of an object relative to grid north, magnetic north, or the boat's direction.

Beat. To sail as close as possible (or close-hauled) towards the wind (about 45 degrees) in a zigzag course.

Berth. Location in a harbour used for mooring vessels, usually alongside a wall.

Beaufort scale. Wind force scale. Light winds are 1–3, moderate 4, fresh 5, strong (or half gale) 6, gale 7+. Ideal sailing winds are 3 upwind, and 4 downwind or broad reach.

Block. Pulley; or blocks, a set of pulleys.

Boom. Horizontal spar at bottom of mainsail.

Boom crutch. Support which holds the boom when not in use; can also support the mast when lowered.

Boat roller. Inflatable roller to allow boat to be hauled across a beach.

Bow. Forward part of boat.

Broach. Losing control with a sharp turn to windward, often heeling heavily and leading to capsize. Occurs when overpowered and/or in large following seas.

Buoy. Floating aid to navigation, often with a light; or for mooring.

Burgee. Flag at top of mast mainly to indicate wind direction.

Cable. 1/10 nautical mile, about 600 feet.

Capsize. Roll over until the mast is in the water, or to 180 degrees.

Catamaran. Boat with two hulls.

Centreboard. Board in the centre of the boat which can be pivoted downwards as a sort of keel to prevent the boat drifting sideways.

Cirrus. High, wispy clouds, often signalling the approach of a depression and worsening weather.

Clipper. Fast, square-rigged sailing ship of the nineteenth century with three or more masts.

Close-hauled. Sailing as close to the wind direction as possible. Sailing as near as possible against the direction of the wind (generally about 45 degrees in a dinghy).

Cockpit. Area in which crew steer and sail the boat, below the deck level.

Course magnetic. Direction of travel, in degrees magnetic.

Cumulonimbus. Thunder cloud.

Cunningham. Line for tensioning the mainsail luff.

Dead reckoning (DR). Navigation technique using direction and distance travelled to estimate position. Often compared to position fixes to check reliability of navigation calculations.

Deep reefed. Reefed to more than a first reef for heavy weather.

Depression. Or **low**. Area of low pressure usually with rain and strong winds around it, anticlockwise in the northern hemisphere. Wave low is a secondary low following the first one on its cold front.

Dinghy. Small, open boat without a keel or cabin.

Downhaul. Line to tension the luff of a sail.

Downwind. Direction that the wind is blowing towards, away from the wind.

Dutchman's log. Float on the end of a line, used to measure speed.

Ebb tide. Falling tide, both height and direction.

EPIRB. Emergency Position Indicating Radio Beacon.

Fair tide. Tidal stream going in the direction of travel. Opposite to foul tide.

Feather. To point slightly higher than close-hauled, mainly to reduce power and heeling.

Fender. Soft bumper used to keep boat from banging into dock.

Flood tide. Rising tide, both height and direction.

Following sea. Wave or waves going in the same direction as the boat.

Foot. The lower edge of a sail.

Foredeck. Deck area in front of the mast, usually wetter and more dangerous location than the rest of the boat.

Foresail. Sail in front of the mast; also headsail, jib or genoa.

Forestay. Wire holding up the mast from the bows.

Foul weather. Strong winds, often with rain.

Freeboard. The height of the deck above the waterline.

Furler. Device to roll up the headsail.

Genoa. Large jib or foresail.

Geographical position. Location on the earth's surface directly below a celestial body, which would then be vertically overhead.

Gimbal. Device to allow swinging, usually a cooker, to keep it horizontal.

Goose-winged. Sails set for downwind sailing, with mainsail on one side and headsail on the other.

GPS. Global Positioning System: satellite-based radio navigation system providing continuous worldwide position fixing.

Gudgeon. Attachment with hole for connecting to a pintle to secure a rudder.

Gunwale. Upper edge of hull.

Gybe. To change direction downwind with the stern of the vessel turning through the wind.

Halyard. Line used to raise a sail.

Headland. Promontory, usually high, with cliffs, on a convex section of coastline.

Headsail. Sail in front of the mast; also foresail, jib or genoa.

Head to wind. Pointing the bow directly into the wind.

Heave to. Stopping a boat by lashing the helm to leeward, with headsail hauled to weather, and the mainsail freed off to leeward, allowing slow drifting to leeward.

Heavy weather. Force 5–6 or more.

Heel. To tip sideways in response to the force of the wind.

Helm. Device for steering a boat (in a dinghy, a tiller). Also the member of the crew who is steering.

Horizontal sextant angle. Angle measured between two objects in a horizontal direction.

Jib. Relatively small headsail, smaller than a genoa.

Jury rig. Emergency rig, usually put together after a dismasting.

Keel. Bottom of a vessel; or heavy weight on the bottom of a boat, or below the hull, often lead, to keep a boat upright and prevent sideways drift.

Keelboat. Boat with a keel, usually a yacht.

Kicking strap, or **vang**. Adjustable wire to prevent the boom rising.

Knot. Unit of speed: one nautical mile (approximately 1.15 statute miles) per hour.

Landfall. Arrival at land after a sea passage.

Latitude. Distance north or south of the equator, measured in degrees.

Lee. Direction away from the wind.

Lee shore. A downwind shore, with a risk of being blown onto it. Opposite of weather shore.

Leech. The aft edge of a sail.

Leeward. In a downwind direction, the direction that the wind is blowing towards.

Leeway. The amount that a boat is blown sideways by the wind.

Lifelines. Lines to prevent man overboard.

Longitude. Distance east or west of the Greenwich Meridian, measured in degrees.

Luff. Leading edge of sail. Foot is the bottom, leech the aft edge.

Luff up. To steer a sailing boat more towards the direction of the wind until the pressure on the sails is eased.

Mainsail. Large sail with boom along its foot and luff along the mast.

Marlin spike. Spike, often on a pocket knife, used on rope work.

Mess tin. Tin used in British Army for storage of food, cooking, drinking, and cleaning.

Mooring. Attachment of boat to a mooring buoy.

Nautical mile. Unit of distance at sea, about 1.15 statute miles (1,852 metres, about 6,076 feet).

Navigation. Process of fixing a boat's position and direction, and calculating how to reach the intended destination.

Navigation lights. A system of lights that a boat must display at night to indicate its position and direction of travel. For a sailing boat, this is a white light aft, a green light to starboard and a red light to port; or for sailing vessels less than 7 metres, have ready at hand an electric torch or lighted lantern showing a white light which shall be exhibited in sufficient time to prevent collision.

Occulting. Light which has dark periods shorter then light periods, the opposite of flashing.

Offshore. Out to sea, or wind direction blowing away from the land.

Offwind. Downwind.

Oilskins. Foul-weather gear, named after clothing used in the nineteenth century made of canvas soaked in oil for waterproofing.

Onshore. Wind direction blowing towards the shore.

On-watch. On duty (helming in a dinghy), usually with a fixed rotation; off-watch is off duty, but on standby.

Outhaul. Line to tension the foot of a sail.

Overcanvassed. Carrying too much sail, and needing reefing or shortening of sail.

Overfalls. Dangerously steep and breaking seas due to strong currents over a shallow rocky bottom.

Phosphorescence. Blue-green light emitted by phytoplankton.

Pilot. Navigation book containing details of passages, weather statistics, ports, navigation aids, not in annual form.

Pintle. The pin or bolt on which a boat's rudder pivots. The pintle rests in the gudgeon.

Plane. To sail faster than hull speed such that the boat rises above its own wash and rides it.

Pooped. Swamped by a high, following sea over the stern.

Port. Left side facing forward. Has red light at night.

Position fixes. Visual, radio, or satellite measurements that enable fixing a boat's position, independently of its dead-reckoned estimated position.

Quartering breeze. Wind from aft of the beam, as in a broad reach.

Radar reflector. Passive device for reflecting ship's radar transmission, to alert the ship by means of a bigger response than from a small vessel.

Radio beacon. Radio transmission beacon which allows homing or approximate direction plotting, up to 200 miles off.

RDF. Radio direction finder, to take bearings of radio beacons.

Reach. Sailing direction with the true wind from 60 degrees to 160 degrees: fine reach with wind slightly before the beam; beam reach with wind abeam; broad reach with wind aft of the beam, but not dead downwind.

Red ensign. Marine flag of British vessels, with Union Jack on a red background.

Reef. Reduction of mainsail area, either by rolling the sail around the boom, or by tying down slabs of sail to the boom.

Reefing claw. Device to allow attachment of kicking strap to a boom with a rolled reef.

Rigging. Wires and ropes usually attached to the mast: standing rigging is that which does not move and generally supports the mast; running rigging is that which moves and usually is for hoisting sails.

Rowlock. Fulcrum device to allow oar to swivel.

Rudder. Steering device located aft.

Run. Sailing direction with the wind from astern, or aft.

RYA. Royal Yachting Association.

Safety harness. Straps worn to prevent man overboard.

Scull. Propulsion by oar from the stern or transom.

Sea anchor. Parachute-shaped device deployed into the water to reduce speed and hold bows head to wind in severe weather. Also para-anchor, a larger version, which stops a boat dead when deployed from the bows; and a smaller drogue, which slows the boat, deployed off the stern.

Sector light. Light with directional information, usually a white sector indicating the correct angle of approach, and red or green sectors to indicate being off course and often in dangerous waters.

Self-bailer. Device for sucking water out of the bottom of the boat at speed.

Sextant. Navigational instrument for measuring angles very accurately, often to better than one minute (1/60 of a degree), usually of a celestial body to the horizon.

Sheet. A rope used to control the setting of a sail in relation to the direction of the wind.

Shipping forecast. Marine weather forecast, mainly used for wind force and direction in sea areas.

Shroud. Standing rigging to hold the mast up from each side.

Sight reduction tables. Marine navigation tables to enable calculation of celestial body position and comparison with measured positions, so as to be able to plot lines of position.

Slack water. Period of no tidal currents at high or low water, between ebb and flood tides.

Spinnaker. Large parachute-shaped sail for sailing downwind on a broad reach or run.

Spinnaker pole. Pole for attaching the tack of a spinnaker to the mast.

Spreader. Metal strut to stabilise the mast.

Spring tide. Strongest and highest tides, when the sun and moon are in line. Opposite of neap tides, when sun and moon are not in line, at right angles to each other.

Squall. Large, dark cloud, usually with strong, gusty winds and rain, sometimes with lightning and thunder.

Starboard. The right side of the boat, facing forward. Denoted with a green light at night. Derived from the old steering oar or 'steer board' which preceded the invention of the rudder.

Statute mile (sometimes called the land mile). 5,280 feet, about 0.87 nautical miles.

Steerage. The effect of the helm on a boat.

Stern. The aft end of the boat.

Stowage. The amount of room for storing materials on board a ship.

Tack. The front corner of a sail. Also a leg of the route of a sailing vessel, with wind on the port side (port tack), or starboard side (starboard tack). Also the process of steering through the eye of the wind to go from port to starboard tack while beating into the wind.

Thwart. A bench seat across the width of an open boat, often where the rower sits.

Tidal race. Area where there are strong and powerful tidal streams, often with eddies and overfalls.

Tidal stream. Flow of tides.

Tide rip. Area where tidal streams are strong and violent.

Tiller. Stick for controlling the rudder.

Transom. Rear or aft end of the boat, at the stern.

Trapeze. Wire and harness for the crew to enable standing in a near-horizontal position outboard of the gunwale, to add extra stability to the boat.

Trimaran. Boat with three hulls.

Trysail. Small storm sail for use instead of the mainsail, attached to the mast.

Upwind. Direction the wind is coming from; or passage into the wind.

Vertical sextant angle. Angle between the top and bottom of an object such as a lighthouse or cliff, to enable calculation of distance off.

VHF. Very high frequency radio, for voice communications at short range.

Warp. Line for attaching a boat to the dock, or to an anchor or mooring.

Weather tide. Tidal stream going against the direction of the wind, causing steep and rough seas.

Windward. Towards the wind.

Acknowledgements

This book is a product of hundreds of people's efforts, first for making the adventure possible, and second for the story. I have mentioned many of them in my narrative, but there were others, unmentioned, to whom I owe gratitude. They did not do it for money, as I was a teenager and had none to spare. They did it because of the excitement – for the adventure of being part of a team that would test the unknown.

I am particularly indebted to David Thomas, who asked me to write the story up for *Yachting World* magazine in 1968. In exchange, I got some crewing on an America's Cup boat. I was inspired and encouraged by Patricia Eve. Original editor Hugh Brazier helped me put my text into much better shape, with a tone reflecting more of our present times than the 1960s, when much of it was first written. Designer Louis Mackay drew the beautiful maps and charts, and edited much of the artwork.

George Greenwood and Barry Hunt-Taylor, who sailed the most on the these voyages, have reviewed and improved the story some 45 years later, and my thanks go to them for their help in this respect, as well as for their companionship in our adventures, so many years ago.

Brian Thompson

Brian Thompson, who wrote the Foreword, raced with me on my 43-foot Grand Prix trimaran *Spirit of England* in the 1990s, winning the Three Peaks Race, the Scottish Peaks Race, and the Azores Race;

together with class wins in the Fastnet Race; and the Round Britain and Ireland Race.

Brian is regarded by many as Britain's top offshore sailor. On *Spirit*, I remember him for his brilliant driving skills, his courage in going up the tall mast in tough conditions for repairs, his experience, and his strategic thinking. He always displayed a logical, positive and unflappable personality: relaxed and confident, but fiercely competitive. He is also modest and unassuming.

Brian became the first Briton to break the Round the World sailing record twice, and the first to sail non-stop around the world four times. He has broken twenty-seven world records, which sets him apart from every other world class sailor on the Grand Prix circuit. He sailed over 100,000 miles with Steve Fossett, breaking many records including the Round the World Record on the 125ft Catamaran *PlayStation*. I was lucky enough to crew once on *PlayStation*. It was exciting, flying a hull at high speed on what was then the world's fastest offshore sailing boat.

Brian has sailed in major solo ocean races, including the OSTAR race, the Route du Rhum and the Vendée Globe non-stop Round the World Race. These single-handed ocean races tax sailors to the limit of their physical and mental capacity, and can only be tackled by people with resilient personalities, top physical fitness, and enormous experience in the harshest of conditions in the open oceans. Much of the time on the Round the World races is in the Southern Ocean, offshore Antarctica, battling hurricane force winds and icebergs.

In 2012 Brian broke the Round the World sailing record for a second time on board *Banque Populaire V*, a 140ft trimaran, crossing the finish line in 45 days, at an average speed of 26 knots. No powerboat or ship has come anywhere near this time. This trimaran has exceeded speeds of 47 knots. This indicates how far technology has come in the last few years, and how much crew skills have been able to develop. Speeds have doubled in the last 20 years. Brian is right up there with the best, setting an example for all of us, not just in sailing, but in pushing the envelope beyond known limits.

About the Author

After the sailing of the 1960s described in this book, Peter Clutterbuck worked offshore on North Sea oilrigs. He later produced *The Sixty Minute Sailor*, a learn-to-sail video, filmed in California using *Calypso*. He became a professional yachtsman, a US Coast Guard licensed captain, and a sailing instructor. Jobs included yacht charters, deliveries, and teaching at an offshore navigation school.

He has sailed off the coasts of all seven continents (if you include kite-skiing in Antarctica!), and has sailed across both Atlantic and Pacific Oceans, including taking part in the Singlehanded Transpacific Race.

Brian Thompson joined him to campaign the 43-foot offshore Grand Prix racing trimaran, *Spirit of England*, to fifteen wins and four international race records, mostly in Atlantic waters. These included the Fastnet Race, the Falmouth–Azores Race, and the Round Britain and Ireland Race.

He has served on the Offshore Racing Council, drawing up international ocean racing safety regulations, and has designed and patented a bow-faced rowing system.

He still sails *Calypso* with his two sons, sailing from Hayling Island on the south coast, where he is also a rescue RIB driver.